Soft

A MEMOIR

Sherrie Fernandez-Williams

North Star Press of St. Cloud, Inc.
St. Cloud, Minnesota

In loving memory of Dorothy Fernandez-Williams, 1935-2014.

Cover design by Coloring Circles

ISBN: 978-0-87839-742-6

First Edition: September 2014

Printed in the United States of America

Published by
North Star Press of St. Cloud, Inc.
P.O. Box 451
St. Cloud, Minnesota 56302

northstarpress.com

"The feminine is more powerful than the masculine, the soft is more powerful than the hard, the water is more powerful than the rock."

–Osho

1

MADISON WAITED at the east entrance of the administration building (which some faculty referred to as the "dark side"), where the offices of the president and the vice-presidents were housed, where students paid their tuition, and new employees signed W-2s. It was an old university structure with ceramic floors and unlevel stairs, named after a saint who found women to be substandard according to some card-carrying feminist theologians. The day we met for lunch seven years ago, Madison stood at the bottom of the landing with her shoulder propped up against the antique-white cinderblock. Her posture was relaxed, but her face told another story. Did she wonder if my purpose for lunch concurred with her purpose? Did she oscillate between her logical left and emotional right? Later, I came to know her as centrist-brained, while I am 99.999 percent heart and gut—therefore, who even needs a brain?

The last time we had met over the noon hour, we were two people working for the same institution, discovering we had a few things in common as two black women born fourteen months apart. We were both raised by single parents in public housing and were both eager to find the hidden tunnel to dig our way out of our circumstances. We both lived inside out, quiet in many settings, but loud while laughing. At first, we were becoming friends. However, the day she waited for me at the bottom of the steps, she seemed almost nervous—strange for a friend to be nervous about meeting another friend for pizza, of all things.

I took a moment to take her in before making my presence known. I'm taller than average and she's taller than I am. Her hair was cut close to the scalp, as it still is today and as it had been before we met, while she was still a graduate student. That day, she wore a black T, loose-fitting khakis, and pair of Air Jordans. Later, I came to know this as her summer attire. During the school year, her daily uniform, as she calls it, consists of dress shirts and laced shoes designed for a gent's sensibility. Dark slacks eventually became dark wranglers after tenure garnered her the right to wear jeans to work. I needed such a gig.

Political types might say her presentation was gender non-conforming. Madison would simply say that her clothes were comfortable and her shoes provided ample support to her arches and ankles. Early on, she wondered if her sensible fashion would be a drawback for me. When I first visited her apartment, she showed me her wardrobe—her button-downs and sports coats. I was insanely attracted to this woman whose rounded edges softened clothing made for square bodies. She was a balanced blend of pretty and strapping, delicate and strong. The day Madison waited for me at the exit of the *big house* and peered out of the small window, I wondered what thoughts emerged as she waited.

Months before our first lunch meeting, Madison spotted me from a distance on the main floor of the foreboding hall. She was there to conduct official business, the only motive anyone would have to enter the shadowy chambers also known as my personal tomb. Unlike Lazarus, I waited more than three days for Jesus to roll away the stone that kept me locked inside and order me to step out.

I had no idea I was being noticed by anyone. My role was not to be noticed. My role was to assist my superior, the executive vice-president, by making certain he arrived at the right meeting at the right time with the correct documents in his hands. Before accepting that position, I underestimated the skill required to perform such a job well. However, after three years trying to be a good assistant, I marveled at those who actually succeeded. Before this, I had been a good advisor at another local college, certainly a more suitable fit for someone with a hunger for human connection. In between the two colleges, I temped my way through short-term assignments within various departments of a medical device company—human resources, brain stimulation, foundations—always completing duties involving tracking data on spread sheets and void of soulful contact. Circumstances pulled me out of my natural habitat, and I wandered through work without a compass for about a thousand days. First, I entered data by day while completing the capstone project for my MFA degree by night. After finishing the MFA, I went back into higher education to coordinate meetings for the numero uno vice-president in exchange for a sense of temporary permanence and decent healthcare benefits.

During my second year at the university, Madison discovered me. She was an untenured gay professor in the sociology department of a Catholic university. I was a rudderless, married mother of twins—mismatched in life and in work. She was a woman who operated with single-minded focus. I inhaled smoldering self-doubt and could easily become sidetracked. She thought my preoccupation upon our first meeting meant I was aloof and uninterested in making new acquaintances. I was in fact distressed, wondering how I might unsnarl myself from the mess of tangles I had woven myself into. Yet the first time we met for lunch in the student cafeteria, she learned that I laughed almost as easily as she did. She learned I could be warm when I wasn't entirely scattered or scared.

Months after the first lunch, that day we met for pizza at the end of July, Madison stood at the bottom of the stairs until I noticed her and called her name. She smiled broadly when I thanked her for waiting and she held the door open for me. She was protective of me, holding her arm out to prevent me from walking in front of oncoming traffic. I wondered if she thought I was incapable of crossing the street without an escort. Previously, we were two women at work who met for lunch a couple of times. All of a sudden, we were weird ladies in our mid-thirties acting as if we were in middle school. A shift happened. I felt graceless in my body. I worried that I should not have worn those open-toe sandals exposing my ugly feet. Eddie Murphy would have said it looked like MC Hammer hammered all over my feet. That was me, ol' Hammertime toes. I tried to cover a snagged thread by folding my hands in front of blue sundress. Did she observe my clumsy non-verbals? Sweaty from anxiety and humidity, my foundation must have melted away. I still hadn't found a good remedy for the dark blotches on my cheeks.

That day over pizza and cola, Madison told me her plan was *not* to be in a relationship.

"I have a five-second rule, and that's all I need."

"What's that?" I asked.

"I see a fine woman, and I allow myself five seconds to take in her beauty, and then I move on."

"Well you know what they say: five seconds can turn into a lifetime." I didn't know who "they" were, but I hoped she caught my drift.

She tried to convince me she meant it. Perhaps she thought because I was a married mother, it was better to behave as friends from work eating pizza. Well, I ate pizza. She had a hoagie without cheese because she couldn't eat dairy. Anyway, she could tell me she didn't want to be in a relationship, and it shouldn't have had any bearing on my life whatsoever. I showed concern.

She talked about her walk as a believer, how a person would be more available to do God's work if they weren't romantically involved.

"Are you sure you can live that way?" I asked.

"I've been living this way for years."

"Really? You don't seem like the type."

She tried to throw me off-course, but Madison's honest nature couldn't help but tell the truth.

"I read one of your essays online."

"Really?" My breathing shortened and hands weakened, my body's immediate stress response before my stomach caved with sickening regret. Previously, I believed if Madison read one of my essays, she would know me better. In person, I was usually careful not to give voice to the random, crazy shit that entered my thoughts, which could be disorganized and sluggish when I was anxious. To avoid appearing feeble-minded, I said little. I was less careful when I was typing. I was soothed by the sound of clicking keys. I could stop mid-sentence, eat a couple of handfuls of raw almonds and dried cranberries and search my surroundings for clarity. *Where the hell did I put the right words? I keep stubbing my toes on the wrong ones.* I could restate, rearrange, and repurpose clichés. I was comforted by the delete function.

"Sherrie," she unfolded her hands and held them in front of her, palms open and eyes wide. "I need you to finish your book."

I was struck by the confession, "I need you . . ." I no longer had to guess how she felt. She said it herself. She needed me.

Madison needed me and within twenty-four hours of her telling me so, I recognized my need in all of this. I needed dear-heart to tie up her ambiguous shoes and walk directly into my life.

What came after the preposition was not inconsequential. We were eating lunch that day, needing each other one year after I completed my MFA degree. I needed to "finish my book" as much as any MFA graduate. In seven words, Madison cast a vision of what our lives would be. It included her charging up my laptop and waking me up on a Saturday morning saying, "It's time to work, love." She wasn't an illusionist. She was the real McCoy—a shaman, or prophetess. Only someone cherished by the supernatural could transform someone's life with a simple string of words—no steamy potion, no abracadabra. What other powers did she possess? I believed in the connectedness of things, people, and places. In an instant, Madison became connected to the significant events of my past. Twenty-four hours after eating pizza, I fell like a 1970s Zenith dropped from a high-rise.

•••

Things I had to have

There have been a few things in life I absolutely had to have. Before my eighth birthday, I was desperate for a skateboard. I saw my brothers and boys in the neighborhood glide on concrete after two giant pushes off the ground. I had to know what it felt like to sail on cement.

There was no set visitation schedule with Daddy. He seemed to surprise us on random evenings before heading home from work. When I was still small, I was quick to run to the door when I heard a knock. Too short to see through the peephole, I learned how to climb on the protruding hinge with my left foot and hold my balance by gripping the knob with my right hand. I perfected this technique as did the seven siblings before me. When I saw Daddy's face made distorted by the thick glass, I would be overjoyed.

"It's Daddy!" He was always just the man I wanted to see. Usually, it was enough to sit close to him and smell his aftershave and have his baritone voice rumble against my eardrums. Nothing calmed my worries as much as experiencing Daddy's presence, perhaps other than shoving my face into my mother's afro while she slept and smelling her blue magic hair conditioner.

I don't have very many memories of Daddy living with us. However, I do remember leaving the room I shared with my sister Gina and squeezing my small frame in between my sleeping parents. I don't know if it was something I did only once or if it was a nightly ritual. I just remember needing to be close to them, both of them. At eight, I developed other needs. At eight, I needed a skateboard. I was absolutely sure of that.

Daddy thought I'd gone completely whacky on him. "It is just too dangerous," he said. Of course it wasn't too dangerous for my brothers, but I was a girl-child in the year 1978, only six years after the enactment of Title IX, which gave girls equal opportunity in public school athletics. Of course, I was noticeably timid, a known scardy-cat, but I had an inner toughness most knew nothing about. I could catch a football and beat people up when their teasing got to be way too much. Who knew these things? Only a few stunned people.

"Please, Daddy. I promise I'll be careful."

I lied to Daddy and told him I already knew how to ride. I practiced on Kyle's. Of course, I only practiced in Kyle's ten-by-eight bedroom, pushing myself from one end of his dresser to the other, but Daddy didn't need to know that. Finally, in response to my persistent pleas, my father gave me that laugh a parent gives to a kid who just made the most ridiculous request ever. The laugh told me there was no way in hell I was getting a skateboard.

During my birthday weekend, my brother Kyle and I went to visit Daddy at his new place, when he and my stepmother were on a temporary break from one another.

"You'll never guess what I got you for your birthday." Daddy came into the living room holding something behind his back. Before I could guess, Daddy revealed the green skateboard with rubber wheels and ball bearings. I couldn't believe it. He really bought me a skateboard. For the briefest moment, I was thrilled. Thrill turned into terror when I realized I would then be expected to ride it. *Shit. What have I done? I can't ride a skateboard. I'm going to crack my head open on that thing.*

"Let's go out and see you ride," Daddy suggested.

"Uh, right now?"

"Yes. Young lady, you begged me for this thing and now you don't want to ride it."

"No. I want to ride it. I can't . . . wait." I swallowed hard and took my gift from Daddy's hands. Daddy, Kyle, and I left his apartment and went outside. Slowly, I put the board down, placed my right foot on the skateboard while my left stayed firmly planted on the concrete. First, I rolled it back and forth with one foot just to get a feel for how the wheels felt against the ground. There was no furniture for me to hold onto, and the patio seemed huge compared to Kyle's box of a bedroom. With the tiniest push, I put two feet on the board and barely moved.

Daddy was sitting and waiting for me to show my skills, but I had none. Most of the movement I made on the skateboard was my swinging arms that tried to grab the air, like thin air was going to save me from falling and busting my ass.

"I thought you said you knew how to ride a skateboard."

"Well . . ." I couldn't tell Daddy I'd lied to him, but that was already obvious.

It was a bright afternoon in June. It was my birthday, and I always felt I had a very lucky birthday. My very cool Dad just gave me the very thing I thought I wanted soooo badly. I had no choice but to figure out how to ride. It started with tiny little pushes and lots of balance checks. Kyle showed me where to place the foot that would remain steady on the board. Eventually, I learned how to balance my weight on the board without lots of twisting and bending at the waist. Soon, I could give myself a bigger push and glide a couple of feet before panic set in. After two days of trying, I finally had it. It wasn't scary. It was just as amazing as I imagined it would be. I could ride a skateboard. I could lean my weight on the back of the board and spin in circles. I could fly down steep hills. I could take spills on cement and grate the skin off my elbows and knees, endure the humiliating laughter of neighborhood kids who thought I was the strangest person on earth. To them, my cuts and scrapes were ample evidence girls had no business riding skateboards. I disliked being laughed at, but not enough to stop riding.

• • •

Scarier things I had to have

Five years after the skateboard, I told Daddy I needed a typewriter because I was going to write a book.

"Are you?"

"Yes."

Near my birthday, I met him in downtown Brooklyn at a shop that repaired and resold used typewriters. However, when I saw the price, I tried to tell Daddy it was okay. I was going to do without.

The typewriter was one hundred, twenty-nine dollars. I would have never requested such an expensive item.

"We'll get this light blue one over here," Daddy said with a booming voice to get the shop owner's attention.

I felt a familiar panic in my body. Daddy was not a wealthy man. I couldn't possibly ask him to waste his money on my frivolousness. Nauseating guilt, combined with intense fear, made me want to buckle at the knees.

"You will use this, right?" My dad asked.

"Yeah. But it's kind of expensive. We don't have to—"

"No, no. We're getting it. I just want to make sure you'll use it."

"I'll use it." I promised.

I climbed on the B37 lugging my beautiful new machine (that came with its own metal suitcase) behind me. I found a seat and waved to Daddy from the window.

My typewriter hummed with life when I plugged in the black cord. Testing the machine, the keys swiftly struck the white sheet of paper.

•••

When it Began

For me, it started with a headache. Not my headache, but Ms. Hirschman's. My third grade teacher was not much taller than her eight-year-old students. She had light brown hippie hair and wore Dashikis with blue jeans, and espadrille shoes. I believed she had a headache that morning because I watched her pop two aspirin and wash them down with a sip of her Tab soda, which was something I saw her do from time to time. She might have been a woman with bad periods like my mother and like me later.

She handed out sheets of yellow paper that looked like they might have been sliced into halves with a paper cutter. She put the remaining sheets on her desk. In large letters, she wrote the word "COMPOSITION" on the board and told us we would be writing one about anything we wanted until it was time for us to go to lunch. If we needed more paper, we should feel free to come up to get more.

I struggled with the first "faint line," just like in Pablo Neruda's poem I came to love years later, probably noticing for the first time how frightening freedom could be, but eventually I came up with something. Soon, I found my hand moving eagerly across the page. I was up for more paper after completing front and back of the first sheet. The bell rang, and it was time for lunch and recess. I begged my teacher to let me stay in class because I wasn't even close to being finished. She looked down at me with a look of indecision as if she was determining what would be more important: to make the skinny child eat something, or to let the silent child speak because, for the first time in her life, she'd discovered she had something to say. She chose the latter and instructed me to come down to the lunchroom when I was done. But I wasn't done by the time lunch was over. When all the children ran screaming into the yard for recess, I was still not done. When the children returned from recess and stood in a long line for gulps of water from our classroom's water fountain, sweating and panting from playing hard, I was still not done. My teacher told me it was time to move on, collecting my scattered sheets.

What came next was even more startling to the girl I was. At the end of the day, my teacher decided she wanted to read my composition to the rest of the class. The class appeared entertained. They laughed when I said something funny, though I never knew I could be funny. Then, Mrs. Hirschman walked over to me, rested her hand on my shoulder, and very quietly said, "Excellent job."

Disbelief still overtakes me when I recall that day and the first time those words were ever spoken to me. I don't have a clue what I was writing about when I was eight, but I would not be surprised if it wasn't far from what I have written about as adult, dabbling in fictional characters who possessed what I lacked.

On my first day of fifth grade, my first day jitters were hard to contain, as usual. Fifth grade would be different from all of the years before. On my first day of school ever, my neighbor Anthony Mojicha was the kind soul who patted the empty mat next to him, inviting me to sit by him during story time. As long as I live, I will never forget his kindness. However, by fifth grade, our classroom was full of kids I had known for years. Most of us lived right across the street from school, in Farragut Projects, located near downtown Brooklyn, providing housing to low-income black and Latino families. A handful of students were bussed in from other areas, like the lovely brownstones of Clinton Hills. Because Dr. Daniel Hale Williams was still a relatively new school, it was attractive to some middle-income families of color who lived outside of the projects. Some were kids of teachers. Bussed-in students were usually higher achieving than those of us from the neighborhood.

In the 1970s and '80s, our teachers were primarily white. More specifically, they were Jewish. There were exactly five black women on the teaching staff. Among them was Ms. Chase. Ms. Chase dressed sharply in skirt-suits which fell just at the knee and thin high-heels the color of plums—never wedges or flats for her dignified feet. She carried her slightly bent hands at her sides while taking small, quick steps on the tips of her toes across the white ceramic tile, glossy enough to see her own reflection on those first days of school. Ms. Chase owned the chalk between her fingers the way a judge owned her gavel, the way a pitcher owned her ball, the way a rider owned her whip.

As an adult, I've wondered what women like Ms. Chase and her sister-colleagues, Ms. Dodson, Ms. Warner, Ms. Miller, and Ms. Peterson, had to stomach to become the professionals they were. They would have come of age at a time when discriminatory practices in education and in every other sector of society were acceptable codes of conduct. Were they affected by the New York City teachers' strikes that pitted the black and Jewish communities against one another? Black communities fought for greater involvement on their district school boards and inevitably fought for cultural representation in public schools. Jewish teachers felt they were being displaced. They argued in favor of hiring tools such as civil service examinations, exams found racially biased by the black community, who felt the largely Jewish teachers' union, was, essentially, fighting against affirmative action. In the epic fights of 1968, the teachers' union won, while the community members, mostly parents of the student body, lost. My own father involved himself in the battle. He was an activist and drug-prevention educator without a bachelor's degree. It occurred before my parents' divorce, and two years before my birth. My parents were raising seven children together in the New York City housing project, which was supposed to be a temporary home while my family worked its way out of poverty. Four years after the incident, my Dad was remarried and my mother was raising eight children in the projects with no chance of working her way out of poverty. Not only was she a poor mother of a large collection of children, she had a sixth-grade education and significant cognitive delays. She turned to welfare as a means of supporting herself and her children.

Ms. Chase and her coworkers pursued higher education and became teachers in a highly competitive market at a time when black women had limited options as to what they could be. I do know there has always been such a thing in this country as the black middle class, and I also know that regardless of what class our folks might have been in, there were always people who treated us as if we didn't belong. For seven hours each day, these women shared the same space with their students of the same racial heritage. However, by fifth grade, I could sense that, in spite of what we had in common, we still lived worlds apart. Their world included bank accounts, motor vehicles, and college degrees.

In all of my years prior to Ms. Chase, my socioeconomic status held little relevance for me. The federal government classified my family as one living below the poverty line. In fact, the government supported my family with a monthly check, food stamps, subsidized housing, and medical benefits. Still, up until fifth grade, I did not claim "poor" as part of my personal identity. I saw those commercials about starving children with skeletal frames and stomachs bloated with hunger. In the fourth grade, Ms. Steinberg placed an orange UNICEF collection box on her desk and asked us to drop loose change into the box, as we were able. My mother gave me dimes, nickels, and pennies to help end hunger.

I defined myself by my individualities. I was shy. I was scared of the dark and of dogs. I was a daydreamer who loved playing with imaginary friends who joined forces with me to save the day against imaginary antagonists. I loved things with wheels, particularly my roller skates and skateboard. I could cartwheel my way across a field of grass without dizzying. I was a sensitive little sister who could easily be made to cry by someone calling me something other than my name: four-eyes or turkey neck, or sometimes even idiot or dumb-dumb. I usually had very little comeback for my older brother. Television was a great escape from random insults, and I particularly loved watching *Happy Days* and *Laverne and Shirley* on Tuesday nights on ABC. What did it mean to say that I was poor when I ate three times a day, had a place to lay my head at night, and had the luxury of watching mindless television before going to bed at a decent hour?

Although fifth grade was a time of strange turning points, life under the fluorescent lighting felt familiar at first. Ms. Chase was new to me, but because I had the tendency to go with the flow the second I was outside the safety of my mother's presence, I expected life as usual. I'd had the same group of friends for years. My report cards usually noted grades above satisfactory, though less than exceptional. Overall, I was "good." I never fought in school nor had I been disciplined for disrupting class in any way.

Fifth grade started out with us kids sitting in rows from one side of the room to the other. That was nothing new. In previous years, our class configuration started out one way, but would soon be redesigned. After the first week of sitting in rows, we ended up in a large rectangle where our teachers could see each of our faces and we could not hide behind the heads of other children. I always thought our teachers didn't place us in permanent seating right away because they wanted to get a sense of where the behavior problems might come from and then sat us accordingly.

Just as in years before, the first two hours of school were devoted to reading and comprehension. Part of the two hours would be spent reading, after which we would answer the questions in the back of the chapter. Finally, we would discuss the text as a class. Although I tended to be quiet, I did participate. Some stories I enjoyed more than others, and in those cases my hand would go up more often. After the first few weeks of school, our classroom was restructured again. Our desks were not lined up in front of the four walls of our classroom, the way I had become accustomed. Instead our desks were pushed together into clusters of six. Instead of just worrying about the one person on the left and the one person the right, hoping neither of those people were one of the class bullies, we were now clustered with five other children, each of them in close enough proximity to cause harm if they wanted.

We each stood at the perimeter of the room as she called our names and pointed out where we would be sitting. From my new seat, I was able to see that my best friends were clear on the other side of the room. Brand new reading texts fresh out of boxes were placed on our tables. Most were burgundy. However, at my table, Ms. Chase put six blue textbooks. We were asked to each take one and write our names in them.

It did not take me long to notice I was in the higher reading group. I was sitting at the table with the "smart" kids. This included three bussed-in kids: Connie and Evelyn, who wore Buster Brown shoes and Kwame, who came to school each day in sweater vests and button-up shirts. Also at my table were Tony Rodriguez and Rolando Silva, who lived in the projects, but not for long. They would stay just long enough for their fathers to purchase houses in Queens. They were little league ball players who were nice looking and well put together in designer jeans and clean, white sneakers. I was the disheveled kid who always grew taller before anyone could afford to replace my shrinking clothes and who wore oddly shaped tortoiseshell glasses, readily identified as "welfare glasses," a marker of poverty. I was placed in the group with the well-groomed high achievers who always scored years ahead on standardized reading and math tests.

We were given the more complicated text because of our "demonstrated ability." As we sat in our cluster waiting for further instruction, lanky Connie with the Buster Brown shoes said to me, "I don't know what you're doing in this group. You're too stupid to be in this group." I knew Connie was right. There must have been some mistake. I wasn't one of the *smart* kids. They knew it and I knew it.

Before this, I was the student who did my best, who put forth effort, who was well liked by my teachers because, generally, I was compliant and did what I was told. It was the temperament I was born with.

Our teacher would work with the larger class before coming to the blue book table. For the first time, my school day would start in a state of panic. My group members always completed the chapter way ahead of me. They would be done answering the comprehension question when I was just beginning it. Luckily, I usually had time to catch up while Ms. Chase worked with the rest the students in the burgundy text. Most of the time, I could finish before it was our turn. However, on occasion, I would skip a question if I were uncertain about the answer, just to complete as many of them as I could.

I had an unlucky day in Ms. Chase's classroom. When she called my name, my body tightened and my heart quickened. I was asked to share my answer for question number seven. Of course, it was the question I skipped. Still, I nervously flipped through the pages of my text, hoping to land upon the answer.

Ms. Chase had a way of letting her students know her patience was running thin. Pursed lips and narrowing eyes gave her away.

"Tell Sherrie which page she should turn to." Of course the rest of the kids knew. Tony reached over and turned to the page and pointed to the passage that held the answer.

"Read, Sherrie."

I obeyed my teacher's instruction and read the passage quietly. I was then asked to read the question again and answer. I read the question, again, but was still unsure of the answer.

Ms. Chase's was now glaring as she began to talk through her teeth. "Girl, if you don't get your behind out of this classroom this very instant . . . so help me." She didn't shout, but she spoke loud enough for the entire class to hear her.

"Get out, and I don't want to see your face until you can answer the question. Do you understand?"

Her directions were clear. I grabbed my book and left the classroom. I had never been asked to leave a classroom before. I had no idea where to go or what to do, so I ran down the hall to the girl's bathroom. I don't remember if I cried. I remember feeling dread. First, I locked myself into a stall and read the passage over again. I'm sure I asked God to help me.

"Sherrie," Natasha whispered my name. "Sherrie, it's me."

I was embarrassed to show my face, but it was Natasha, my best friend who never judged me. Natasha, who was not in my reading group, was holding a bathroom pass although she really didn't need to go. She just wanted to see if she could help me. I gave her a shot. I showed her the passage where Tony said the answer was supposed to be. However, it was hidden from Natasha as well.

"I'm sorry, Sherrie."

"It's okay."

"I don't know why she had to send you out of the classroom. She is such a bitch. Don't let her bother you." Natasha offered as a word of encouragement. Natasha soon left and I stayed in the bathroom, not sure of what to do next.

Fifth grade was a time of bizarre changes.

Ms. Chase discovered what the other teachers before me were either unable to detect, or were too kind to share. I was a very stupid little girl. It began to feel like I was selected to be on my teacher's shit-list. Ms. Chase got so frustrated with me. She yanked one of my ponytails or pushed the hard nail of her index finger against my temple as she scolded me for being such an idiot. Corporal punishment had been outlawed by then, although Ms. Chase still found a way to poke, yank, and grab her students when she wanted to make a point.

I was quickly moved out of the "brainy" group, and instead of being in the burgundy reading group with the rest of my fifth grade class, I joined Ms. Peterson's fourth grade class for reading. Throughout all of my elementary school years, I'd always tested at my grade's reading level, but I wasn't going to protest. Each morning, I took my new fourth grade textbook and went next door. Ms. Peterson was still as laidback as I remembered her to be. My time with her was completely without stress. The book was easy, and I flew through the questions with little effort. My mornings were completely void of the sound of terror pounding against my eardrums.

Ms. Peterson was convinced fourth grade reading was not a challenge for me and that I needed to go back to Ms. Chase. Ms. Chase was reluctant to take me back, but she did so anyway. Of course, I wouldn't go back to the blue text with the bussed-in kids, but joined the mass of average students with whom I belonged. They were students like me, from the projects, who did not play organized sports or speak standard English, and were despised by our teacher. We were all people of color. However, differences existed between those who were poor and those who appeared not to be. Those who were poor were treated as nuisances who would never amount to anything. Those who seemed to have come from financially stable families were academic all-stars and were treated with respect. They did not have to fend off daily abuse from our teacher. I could not get lost in the crowd. Although I had rejoined the masses, I was still not removed from Ms. Chase's gaze. There was a bull's-eye on my psyche, and she could shoot me there every time.

For a writing assignment, I found a biography on Phillis Wheatley in our school library. The fragile slave girl in poor health soon became my first heroine. Like all of the other book reports and compositions written for Ms. Chase, she marked the word "POOR" in large red writing. Whatever flame my previous teachers were able to spark in me was doused during my time with Ms. Chase, who was black like me, and who I assumed knew me best because of it. My dumb ass was doing nothing but taking up space and my teacher's precious time.

• • •

Fallen Apart

At the end of the year, I still managed to test at grade level on my standardized exams, which meant I would be promoted to sixth grade. I wanted to praise God for allowing me to survive my year with Ms. Chase. Until the rumors started that one of the sixth grade teachers was leaving our school, and in the reshuffling process, Ms. Chase would be moving to sixth grade along with the students.

"God in heaven. Please say it isn't so?" In hearing it was true, I experienced one of those moments in my life when I seriously questioned God's existence or was beginning to believe I was being forsaken.

I continued to frustrate Ms. Chase and she continued to exasperate me. I remained compliant but found other ways to rebel. My attendance went south. I missed a lot of school with one ailment or another. Once, I convinced my mother I might have had the mumps, although she knew darn well I was vaccinated. Sleeping became difficult. Often, I stayed awake most of the night. At 3:00 a.m., I would turn on the small black-and-white television in my room left behind by my older sister and watch *Dr. Ben Cassey*. If only I got so sick I had to be hospitalized like one of Dr. Cassey's patients, I would never have to see Ms. Chase again. In the dead of winter, I opened my windows and shivered in my bed. If I could give myself the sniffles, or better yet, pneumonia, I would escape the hell that was sixth grade. On occasion, I would make myself throw up in the bathroom and then show Ma the evidence that I was not well enough to go to school. I had already been a finicky eater and was thin because of it. Now, my eating was worse than it had ever been. Often, my knees would give out, and I would find myself on the floor in a blink. My mother took me to the doctor, who then scolded her for neglect.

"She's malnourished. Don't you feed her?" the medical doctor in the white coat asked accusingly of my poor mother, who used every tactic imaginable to try to get me to consume food.

"She won't eat!" my mother tried to explain.

I wasn't starving myself on purpose. My already small appetite had gotten smaller, and I continued to make myself vomit to prove I was sick. Later, I heard terms like anorexia and bulimia, and learned about young girls who were dying to be thin. I didn't want to be thin. I wanted to be home. I wanted to be safe.

Relief came in the form of jury duty. Ms. Chase was gone for at least two weeks. Instead of getting a substitute, our class was distributed among the other sixth grade teachers. For two weeks, I sat in Mr. Gappleburg's classroom. Mr. Gappleburg's classes were known for putting on fantastic plays written or adapted by Mr. Gappleburg himself. My favorite was *Oliver and Olivia Twist.* He gave Oliver a twin sister because he wanted a boy and a girl to share the lead.

During my time with Mr. Gappleburg, we wrote lots of essays and shared current events. We always had to include who, what, where, when, why, and how. He pinned my work on the bulletin board with gold stars. His approval confused me, but I delighted in it.

Upon Ms. Chase's return, long and unpleasant days persisted as I suffered one made-up or self-inflicted illness after another. I remember telling Ms. Chase one day I would not be in school the next day because I had to go to "Face to Face" with my mother. It sounded official. My mother had official business, and I needed to go with her. I did not realize that "Face to Face" was actually the welfare office in downtown Brooklyn. Ms. Chase gave me that look she normally gave me when I answered a question incorrectly, or said something asinine. Then came that look of disgust. Years later, I wondered what was her biggest problem with me. Was it that I was on welfare or that I didn't have the good sense to hide it?

I'm not sure what my attendance record was in the sixth grade, but I'm certain I was absent as many days as I was present. I knew it was over—my life, I mean—the day Mr. Gappleburg came to our classroom to see if Ms. Chase would select students from her class to write their reflections about their years at our elementary school.

These narratives would be compiled and offered as gifts to all the graduates leaving our school to face the horrifying halls of junior high. Though Mr. Gappleburg spoke softly near the door during his impromptu teacher-to-teacher conference, I knew he was speaking about me. All of this happened in slow-moving frames, which is why I can still see the details I have played in my head for years. Mr. Gappleburg gave me several quick glances out of the corner of his eye as he spoke to my teacher. I remembered the gold stars he gave me. How could I not? He was definitely there for me.

I stared at the back of Ms. Chase's head and tried to will her face to turn to me. *Please see me for once.* And then I saw it: the back of her head, the two-inch afro turning, her pursed lips and critical gaze caught my look of desperation. "Say yes," I begged with my eyes. "Please." Afraid to smile, I think I couldn't help but smile because for once she was going to see I might be more than a dumb ass. I might actually have something to say. However, her look of consideration faded into something closer to *"no fucking way."*

Turning back to Mr. Gappleburg, I watched her shake her head. "No one here," she said.

• • •

Back together again

At the end of sixth grade, I still scored at grade level on my reading and math standardized exams. This meant I would be promoted to junior high school.

Those of us from Farragut Housing walked the extended block along the defunct Brooklyn Navy Yard to reach McKinney Junior High, the school just outside of Fort Green Housing. My passive nature worried folks who cared about me. It was predicted I would lose my life at McKinney. Some punk-eating ruffian from Fort Green would swallow me whole.

The disorder I encountered in Mr. Martinez's homeroom was expected. I was placed in seven-three, which meant that I was in the third of four tracks. Seven-one was supposed to be the most capable students. Seven-two was considered average. Seven-three would have been less than average, and seven-four was considered the least capable.

I remember walking past seven-one and noticing the order of the classroom. No balled-up sheets of paper were being thrown from one side of the room to the other. The room was clean and quiet. There was no shouting and cussing and kids talking about somebody else's ugly, fat, or stupid momma. I figured the kids in seven-one were on a different path from the kids in seven-three. The students in seven-one were on their way to college and good-paying jobs. If lucky, the students in seven-two would one day be hired by the students in seven-one. I imagined those of us in seven-three would never make it to college and would cope with life as minimum-wage earners. What did that mean for seven-four? Welfare or jail? We all knew what the numbers one, two, three, and four signified. I was seven-three, which meant Ms. Chase was right about me. I wouldn't amount to much and would likely be poor for the rest of my life.

Up until seventh grade, I had been tracked by New York City public schools as an average student with average ability; in other words, a number two. After my two years with Ms. Chase, I was now considered less than that. This is what it meant to be number three at McKinney Junior High.

For the rest of my life, I would always remember Mr. Fracarro. Now that I'm an adult, I refer to him as Frank although I haven't seen or talked to my seventh grade English teacher since I left junior high school.

When Frank returned one of my first assignments, he asked me a question that would alter my life's path forever. "Do you know you're very good at expressing yourself on paper?"

I remember the question. I don't remember my answer, or if I answered him at all. Knowing the girl I was back then, I probably said nothing.

Mr. Fraccarro told us about an annual contest that he facilitated each year with all of the seventh graders. Each class would be represented by four of their classmates. In order to be a class representative, we first had to compete against our classmates. Our class was broken into newscast teams, just like on the nightly news. Each team member was asked to write about something newsworthy and pertinent to our lives as junior high school students. We would then sit at a long table in front of the rest of the class and deliver our story. There were categories: two students wrote about current events, one person covered sports, and I decided to take commentary, which meant I was allowed to provide my opinion on anything I viewed to be an issue at our school. Winners from each category would then compete with the other seventh grade English classes. The winning team's entire class would miss a day of classes for a movie and a pizza party.

The judges were the principal, the assistant principal, the school librarian, and district thirteen's superintendent. My only goal was to not embarrass myself in front of those important people. I tried different topics and decided to go with the cheesy topic of school vandalism. I realize now I played it safe. I hadn't even considered the deeper angst I felt as a young person growing into a woman's body and being propositioned to give some guy with droopy-eyes a blowjob for money. If I knew what I know now, I would have used the platform to speak out against the boys who groped my ass in the lunch line, or the one who hurled basketballs at me in gym class because I was uneasy around him and he took that to mean I was stuck up.

Nope, it was going to be vandalism. Still, I gave my safe topic all I could given the limitations I felt speaking in front of the entire seventh grade, other teachers, and some folks I had never seen before. After my teammates delivered their stories, I delivered my commentary against school vandalism with as much gusto as I could. After all of the teams were done, we sat and waited for the results. The announcement came from our school principal, Ms. Mosely.

"In first place . . . Class seven-one!" Cheers erupted from the top class as they found themselves, yet again, at the top. While seven-one continued to rejoice in their victory, it was announced that class seven-three took second place. Second wasn't bad. I was very accustomed to being a number two, and it sort of felt right.

As my teammates and I congratulated each other on doing better than what was expected of us, Mr. Fracarro summoned me to the judges' table.

Ms. Mosely extended her hand to me as the other judges offered approving smiles.

"We want you to know, Sherrie, that on the individual scores, you were the only person to get a perfect score from each of the judges. You've done a wonderful job."

Who knew that seventh grade would be a time of magic? I could have never predicted things to turn out the way they had. The next day, Mr. Fracarro told me I deserved to be celebrated as much as anyone, so he invited me to attend the movie and pizza party with the winning class.

"Would you like to invite a friend from your class to join you?" he asked me. I was relieved because I didn't have any friends in seven-one.

Although it had rained early that morning, it turned out to be a gorgeous day when Tina Patterson and I met the kids from the winning class outside of the school building as Mr. Fracarro completed his headcount. We were all there and ready to go.

Not surprisingly, Mr. Fracarro had become my favorite teacher, and English my favorite subject. However, my grades improved in every subject, and I made honor roll each quarter. In some ways, I had developed some obsessive study habits, and some might say this period of my life was the start of some perfectionistic tendencies. I didn't think about any of that at the time. I enjoyed the results of my work. My reading scores went up two years during the seventh grade and by the next academic year, I was placed in eight-one. In eight-one, my reading scores went up another two years. In nine-one, my reading score went up another two years, and I knew without a doubt at that point I was college bound. I wanted to have a bank account, a motor vehicle, and a college degree, like my teacher Frank, who seemed to think it was possible for me. I wanted to encourage young people to believe in themselves, so they too could succeed in life.

All the while, my two years with Ms. Chase were never far. Every exam taken and every paper written was an attempt to scrape her words from my psyche. However, even now, she sticks to my memory like burnt cheese. She is forever afixed to my ten-year-old self, who has never had the opportunity to have the adult conversation I'm capable of now. If I could hear her story, would that change my view of her?

In one 1968 article I read on the black/Jewish conflict that pitted poor blacks against Jewish teachers, the writer opined that the parents of the black students were advocating on behalf of children who did not belong in school in the first place. What about Ms. Chase? Would she have agreed with those who believed some children had no business in school? Did she think of me because I wore my poverty in plain view? Or did she believe if she were stern with me, I would snap out of my daydreaminess and become more alert and tough-minded, like a soldier in enemy territory? Would

I have responded to Mr. Fracarro's approval and encouragement in the same way if I hadn't experienced the intense disapproval of Ms. Chase? Water tastes best when we're thirsty. By the time I met Mr. Fracarro, I was brittle and crumbling into small pieces from lack of moisture.

I exert significant energy toward combatting self-doubt. I will catch myself reliving my time with Ms. Chase, remembering how humiliation felt in my ten-year-old body after being sent out of her room because I wasn't good enough to be there. Often, I'm given some reprieve from the fight. Life provides me with moments when I'm surrounded by people who are now what Frank had been to me at age twelve. My mystical teachers, in and out of the classroom, lift my face from the cracked earth and nourish me with living water until I am soaked.

• • •

In the seven days after Daddy bought me my typewriter, I typed one hundred, twenty-nine pages, a page for every dollar my dad spent on my gift. My protagonist was a bold fifteen-year-old swept up in a forbidden romance, as seen on TV—my primary medium of choice.

In 1989, Julia Markus, author of *Uncle*, reminded her class of beginning fiction writers that there was nothing new under the sun. "The sooner you realize that, the better off you'll be," she said. Still, in the years to come, I stretched beyond my limits as if I was capable of razzmatazz.

I wrote about something I knew nothing about. The story was based on the rape of a Central Park jogger, when the public still believed five teenagers of color were guilty of the crime. Later, we found out the public was wrong, the media was wrong, the NYPD was so very wrong. Still, in my wrongness, I imagined one of the young men involved in the rape did not want anything to do with it. He tried to stop the other guys, but they wouldn't listen to him. I described him as "oak-brown." Dr. Markus gave me a C-, which made me rethink my plans.

"What do you know about being a rapist?" she asked me during her office hours.

In my next short story, I wrote about a young woman who was slowly cracking up. I might have been inspired by *The Yellow Wallpaper,* which we read in English Comp. My protagonist was drawn to the color orange. I heard in my psych class that orange provoked emotional disturbance. Later, I learned orange was also the color of creativity. Orange was my favorite color.

"Much better," Dr. Markus wrote on my paper. Dr. Markus said I would be better off writing about something familiar, so I wrote about a young woman with some sort of mood disorder who loved the color orange. Later, I wrote about an overly self-conscious teacher who hated teaching but wanted to make a difference. Again, Dr. Markus felt I was showing improvement. Next, I wrote about a college student in a dishonoring relationship with her boyfriend. When my classmates wrote personal notes to me encouraging me to leave the guy, I thanked them with a chuckle and tried to convince them my story was a work of fiction. Later, I would tell the stories of the same boyfriend, who became my husband, and admit that it was the truth.

Thirty-three years after Daddy purchased that typewriter, that day with Madison at the pizzeria, she could not have known where I would take her words. I took them back to Brooklyn, where I grew up in Farragut Housing. I took them with me to Ms. Chase's fifth-grade class. I took them with me to the inner-ring Minneapolis suburb to the home I purchased with Gregory. I took them with me to work in the administration building of the university and believed I could change my circumstances.

2

I WAS GUSHING with hope over the six days following lunch with Madison. With a week off from work, I devoted hours to linking the places, people, and events responsible for placing me in that moment when my path crossed with Madison's. When I wasn't at the neighborhood coffee shop of our first-ring Minneapolis blackburb, I wrote in the basement of the home I shared with Gregory and our six-year-olds, JB and Jodi. We had painted the basement the color of cooked chickpeas. The sofa and loveseat handed down from Greg's mom drizzled fire tones on top of puffy taupe surfaces. Burnt orange and deep reds ornamented tables and shelves. The brown leather sofa found at an office furniture sale anchored the space. Bookshelves full of textbooks and novels from two sets of undergraduate and graduate degrees gave height to the assemblage of furniture. As I made decisions about what to put where, I envisioned the lower level of the house on Thurber Road being used for some community purpose, perhaps writing workshops or a book club, women making themselves comfortable and munching on treats from a bakery, since I never claimed to be a baker.

I was up at 6:00 a.m. the morning after having lunch with Madison. I no longer worried about waking Greg, who slept in the office. Although JB and Jodi were awake in their beds, they would only leave their shared room to use the bathroom. Otherwise, they stayed contained in the bedroom until Greg said it was time for them to get up. Only then would they quietly stir about, minding their manners so as not to be scolded.

On Saturday mornings, I worked undisturbed for a couple of hours before hearing the voices of Greg, JB, and Jodi above me. On a good morning, there might be laughter.

During the adoption process four years earlier, it was not lost on me that I was going to be raising black children with erratic beginnings, who had lived in five different homes before coming to us. Considering the possibility their self-worth might one day come into question, my intention was to have them believe, to have them be armored with the breastplate of faith, and to have them so convinced of their magnificence that doubt would never linger long enough to enter their marrow and brittle their bones. Certainly, I lived with doubts of my own and had long since mislaid my child-like faith, but I did not want to taint Jodi and JB's innocence with even a speck of their new mommy's skepticism. They were already older than most other nearly three-year-olds because they had already come to understand the adults who were supposed to care for them could be straight-up fickle. Grown folks had the propensity to leave and never return. Grown folks could easily say they loved you, but, like my writing professor said, "Love is a word with little love in it." Love is a word that needs more words and deeds to define it.

I had the desire to be loving toward my children. But I also recognized my tendencies to forget important appointments, lose energy, lose patience, and self-indulge in private woes I chose to make public. Pre-twins, I was able to get by on the minimal amount of energy bestowed on my collection of tired-out cells. Motherhood, however, required much more than what my body was willing to generate. I operated in a state of partial awakeness. I understood that some days I would resent the fact these young ones were so in need of my care, but in those earliest days I could honestly say I heaved the weight of this mission up off the ground with determination to hold it securely in my arms for as long as I possibly could. If I needed to set it down, I pledged I would do so gently. Before their arrival, I felt I had been given the capacity to be a "good" mother but never fully broke down the specific elements incorporated into loving a dependent child. It was all fairly mystical, and I assumed that, once the children came, the necessary elements would breeze through me like whispers. Instinctively, I would be guided on the path of good.

The lesson given in Proverbs that speaks of planning for good reappeared to me during my initial days of parenting. "Plan for good, and then . . . you will find love and faithfulness." I noticed all that was required of me in order to have good in my life. This must be to what L'Engle meant when she said we are co-creators with God. Human effort needed to be extended, sweat glands activated, thought stimulated . . . and then, we would find love and faithfulness.

When they first arrived, I put the preschoolers into the shopping cart and tooled around Toys 'R' Us, wanting to put to use the gift certificate I received from co-workers. "No mindless toys," I said to myself, because I was planning for creative minds. This particular trip I focused on art supplies, finger paint, an easel and painters' smocks, along with glitter glue, Play-Doh, and all of the accessories. I took time off work to establish a kind of "new family orientation." The twins now had a mother, and the mother had her walking and talking baby boy and girl. I found smiley-faced stickers and remembered what I read about positive reinforcement having greater long-term impact than negative. One night, when the children were sleeping, I pulled out markers and large sheets of cardstock, one for each child. On the pink sheet, I wrote at the very top the words, "Jodi Is a Good Girl," and taped it at the head of her bed. I did the same for JB on the yellow sheet. By this time, I discovered what each of their struggles had been. Jodi was not fond of napping, so I thought I would place a sticker on her board each time she took her nap. JB could be possessive of his things, so when I caught him sharing, I would sticker his behavior chart. The modern parenting experts say to catch your children doing the right thing and offer them immediate praise, because it goes further than punishment. They both got stickers for being especially kind to one another. They both received stickers for eating their vegetables, though Jodi had little problem with eating vegetables or any other type of food.

At home, we danced. I did not know my mother's father, who died when Ma was just a little girl of four, the age I was when my parents divorced. Still, I'm convinced my grandfather is the reason why Afro-Cuban rhythms have settled themselves into my knee joints, which direct my hips, not the other way around. It has always seemed to me that people who struggle with Latin movement are not connected to their knees. Instinctively, the knees know what to do. They know how to carry and shift one's weight in time with the heartbeat of the music, the drums of Mother Africa. This is fused with Latin trumpets, which to me are like the amygdala, the part of the brain that lights up when we experience intense emotion. I wanted to see if my children could feel this in their bones, heart, and head when I turned up the volume and tried to teach them basic Salsa steps. They giggled as they moved their small bodies uncontrollably. *Perhaps later*, I thought. Later, however, it was *pop and lock* that drew them where the focus seemed to be isolation of joints in muscles, largely in the upper body. This language, my body had never learned to speak.

I purchased art supplies and tried to determine if somewhere in their two-year-old bodies lived two little thirsty artists wanting to be quenched. We took trips to the library. *Get them to love books early*, I thought. *If they love them early, they will love them for life.* Who doesn't love watching a child in that state of fascination? I wanted to nurture that human need for story, so they might go to that place any time they should need it. I wanted them to be inspired to travel the world of ideas, to land upon their own big ideas, their own passions. A child who never learns to dream is like a missing child. Her photo will never show up on the gumball machine at the grocery store, or as mail addressed to "the resident of . . . ," but she is most certainly missing.

My kids marched around with me—I mean really marched, with knees up in the air, elbows bent, and hands formed as fists. "I have a good brain!" And they would repeat after me. "I am smart! I have a good heart . . . And God loves me!" I guess it was something close to lunacy, but the mission had been set before me. The twins would shout after me, and when we were done, we would fall to the ground, giggling, before beginning our next activity.

Once at the children's section of the library, an older mom with a slightly older child sat beside us as we booted up an *Arthur* story on the PC. She gave us a warm hello and got her little girl started on her computer.

"I have a new mommy," Jodi said to the woman.

"You do?"

I smiled at the woman.

My approach with the children was to structure our time with arts and crafts, readings, or scheduled outings.

Greg's play would usually require him to transform into a fictional character. Sometimes, he would be Mr. Hop-Along, the man-sized bunny. The kids would hop behind him and they'd all look like three Peter Rabbits. Or the Tickle Monster would appear with a blanket over his head and an arm stretched before him like a mummy. The kids knew this meant run as fast as they could and hide. This play would go on forever. Once caught, the Monster pulled the children into his den and tickled them without relenting. The first time the Tickle Monster arrived on the scene, he roared loudly and caused JB to cry in terror. I swooped JB up and said, "Daddy is just being silly. He just wants to play with you." Soon, JB understood and played along, taunting the Tickle Monster, then running away with his sister to find a place to hide. Sometimes, Jodi and JB would find blankets and became miniature Tickle Monsters themselves. They would speak in their scariest voices, mimicking the ghost of Christmas Past. "We are looking for Daddy. He must come with us, now . . ." As they got closer, Greg would roar loudly. The kids would scream and run away.

Other times, Greg would be Mr. Oz from planet Boz. The kids adored wonderful Mr. Oz. Although he was from another planet, he spoke with an English accent. He would often appear at our house on Saturdays around the lunch hour. Mr. Oz knew nothing of planet earth, and it was up to the children to help him function in his new home. He did not know how to properly use eating utensils or make a telephone call. Of course, he didn't know that the people on television could not hear him talking to them.

The children took great pleasure in helping Mr. Oz get acquainted with their new home. Every so often they would question Mr. Oz.

"Are you really our Daddy?"

Mr. Oz would always deny this. "I would love to meet your Daddy someday. I heard he is very handsome."

"You look like our Daddy," one of them might say.

"Yes, well, everyone on Boz looks just like some person on earth."

"There's somebody who looks just like me? Really?"

It was rare for the four of us to play together. Greg played with the kids in his way. My activities were less organic. I was all about routine and minimizing chaos. I was the one who took time away from work in those early days of parenting and was on duty twenty-four hours a day. Greg played and left, always having so much to do at work.

I learned that I needed to be systematic and prepared for everything. Originally, I would wake around seven, wake the children, prepare breakfast for them, then make my way to my closet to figure out what I was going to wear. By this time, I was fifty pounds down and finding clothes that fit was a task in itself. I desperately needed to go shopping, but I was a mother of twins now, and my children were always with me. I was not skilled enough to navigate shopping for women's clothing with the children along.

After finding the same sweatpants and sweatshirt that I'd worn almost every day that the children were home with me, it was time to take a shower. I put up the protective gate at the bedroom door. I then proceeded to tell the children that Mommy would return shortly, that I needed to take a shower. I would plead with them to play nicely. "Remember, no jumping on the bed," I would tell them, thinking that to have the children crack their skulls while I was in the shower would be all I needed. They would look at me with their arms hanging over the gate. "Okay, Mommy," they would say. I would bribe them with treats: "if you want a treat when I'm done, then you'll play nicely and share your toys." "Okay, Mommy," they would say. About three minutes into my shower, I'd hear the call that would become all too familiar. "Stop!" Then, "Mommy!" Then wailing. Out I would jump, wet in my towel. JB, still with tears in his eyes, looked up at me and began laughing, with tears falling on his cheeks.

"What!? What's so funny?"

"You're soapy," followed by more giggles.

"Look," I said. "All I want to do is take a shower. Is that too much to ask?"

"No," they would say.

"Nobody's getting a snack. I said you had to play nicely. Why was JB crying?!" I asked, directing my question to Jodi.

"I don't know."

"JB, why were you crying?"

"Jodi hit me."

"Jodi, did you hit JB?"

"Yes."

"Why?" The answer would be the same. She wanted to play with one of JB's toys, and JB wouldn't let her.

After showering, I would warm up the hot roller and spend thirty minutes before the mirror trying to make myself presentable for the world outside my door. And it wouldn't be until after this that I'd begin making the children presentable. And in the early days "presentable" meant not just neatly dressed, but cutely dressed with a subtle attempt to coordinate the twins' clothing, although sometimes it would not be as subtle.

One day when we were meeting our friends at the zoo, we were finally ready to grab our coats when I smelled something. I got closer to my Pampers-less children to find which one made the stink. This time it was Jodi.

The children came to us potty trained and in the process of them coming to us, they had become un-potty trained. "You can't sweat these things," I told myself, although I was sweating and felt my blood pressure rising. I called my friend to tell her that we were going to be even later than I thought. This was now the third phone call extending our meeting time. My friend and mother of three children, who by then were seven, nine, and eleven, was kind to me, saying, "You'll get it figured out soon enough." Now, I know she must have been laughing at me, as I have later sympathetically chuckled at new mothers losing their grip.

Each day I learned something new. I learned children won't fight over a toy if they no longer have it in their possession. The rule had become, "If you're going to fight about it, who gets it?" I would hold out my hand and one of the children would place it there, answering, "Mommy gets it." Then one or the other would perk up and say they wouldn't fight about it anymore. The toy would be returned and magically they kept their promise not to fight about it. I learned not to give the children mashed potatoes because they simply didn't like it. They did, however, like rice, so I give them rice. One battle had been prevented. I learned that a bath at night made them sleepy. I learned it wasn't necessary to read the book they thought they wanted you to read. I read the book I knew they'd be glad I read, once I had read it. Longer stories made them sleepy, though they never appeared to be bored. I learned they relaxed when I sang to them and rubbed their backs at the same time. So at night I did these things and they were happy to say "Goodnight, Mommy," roll over, and stay there until the next morning when I woke them.

Thirty days at home getting to know my children. I spent my days always thinking ahead of the moment. My goal was to leave the house everyday. I found that, when I took the children out each day, it made the days go by faster. I'd take them out, before or after a nap. I would bundle them up good. I'd take them to the park down the street where the jungle gym seemed just a bit too big for their two-year-old legs. I discovered the "Playplace" at McDonalds and found the combination of Chicken McNuggets and sliding down a plastic tunnel made for cooperative children. "If you clean your entire room and pick up all of your toys and books, we'll go to play at McDonalds." Efficiently they would move, picking up every single Lego block, every single crayon that'd been stepped on and broken into five pieces. Every doll was deposited to its proper spot. Every book stacked neatly on the shelf, standing up the way Mommy showed them.

"We're done. Can we go to Play McDonald's now?" I would inspect the work and inevitably say "Yes, we can go now." I learned that my own morning routine needed to be shortened or I needed to wake up earlier. And then I discovered both were true. First, I would wake up an hour earlier, get myself showered and ready to take on the team. The team would be ready to rock as soon as the door of their bedroom opened and I said the words, "It's wake-up time!" They'd hop down and make their way to separate potties.

We'd return from our afternoon's activity: the library, the park, the zoo, the "Play McDonalds." It would be time for a nap. I'd turn on *Dr. Phil* in the living room and cook dinner in the kitchen to make two separate meals, one for Jodi and JB, one for Mommy and Daddy. Daddy would arrive and eat his dinner and run. Just as he had been running out all summer long, even now that the children were with us. He was still running. Off to make the doughnuts but, by now I was completely sick of it, but again . . . tight job market . . . gotta do what you gotta do.

• • •

JB was a boy made of one-hundred-percent confection. My prayer was that he stayed who he was created to be. He was thin but not frail, with an enormous tolerance for pain and discomfort. We called him the rubber boy because of the way he flung his body to the ground and sprang back up again. He was quite willowy, and was an aspiring dancer. With his long eyelashes and pleasant little face and thin body, he was fond of walking on the very tip of his toes with arms out and over his head as if he is being lulled by his own movement. If anyone asked him what he wanted to be, he told them he wanted to dance. He told them he was an amazing dancer. Once, after picking him up from preschool, he asked me if I thought he danced like a girl. I asked him why and he told me that Christian, another preschooler, laughed at him and said he danced like a girl. I told him I thought he danced beautifully and that it brought me to joyful tears when he moved the way his heart guided him to.

• • •

Jodi watched her brother and applauded. "Yay, JB . . . Go, JB!" Jodi no doubt was the woman I dreamt about before adoption became reality. Although it was a dream, I knew everything there was to know about her. I was proud of the woman she had become, confident and full of love and care for what was good. She was full of love for me, and I remembered feeling a sense of unworthiness for this adoration. It astonished me that what I had wished for in children years before I would receive—a sensitive son and a strong-willed daughter. I believed Jodi would take on the creeps of this world. My baby girl . . . and of course, when I called her that, she smiled with her face and body. She delighted in my praises.

She was not built like her brother. She was taller and thicker, with bigger hands and feet. People told me girls developed faster than boys, which was why there was the size difference between my twins. But Jodi was developing faster than the average girl. We took her to a specialist, an endocrinologist, to get her tested in order to find out if she needed medication to slow down her development. The fear was if she developed too quickly her height could be severely stunted. They drew blood and found that she would be just fine. We were told that black girls developed at faster rates than children of other ethnicities. She already had womanly curves, and her dad worried she would attract the wrong kind of boy when she got older. My fear was that, when she got older, she would not appreciate the beauty she was blessed with. At almost six, she would tell me she wished she was skinny like her brother and sob into my lap because she could no longer fit into her favorite fancy pants and because a boy at school called her fat. I told her she was beautiful, but that didn't console her. I cursed the world that would give my child a body image complex at five.

•••

What concerned me most regarding our little girl was not really her size, or the fact that she was already having crushes on boys. I declared my love to a boy at the age of five and to this day, I might argue it was the best relationship I ever had with a guy. We laughed, we played, and never once did we exchange a harsh word to one another. What concerned me about my daughter was her watchfulness in grownup matters. Others saw this too. Once, when the twins were three and a half, the three of us were sitting on the bus heading for the state fair grounds. We sat next to a kindly gentleman in his senior years who'd lived in this town his whole life. I knew because he told us. He also told me he and his wife had nine children. As he spoke, Jodi listened with full attention, never taking her eyes off the friendly elder. In the middle of his speech he peered into Jodi's face, as Jodi peered back at him.

"She's a smart one, isn't she?

"Yep," I responded.

"I can tell."

I and others have come to the conclusion that Jodi was only one part child. She frightened her daddy with her perceptiveness. Often at night, Greg crept into Jodi and JB's room to see if they might be awake. Though he had not been around a great deal in those early days, it was clear to me that she was becoming something close to royalty to him and he was becoming the great man in her life. He found our insomniac daughter awake with her eyes clear and bright in the darkened room.

"Hi, Daddy," she would say.

"Hi, little girl . . . whatcha doin' up?"

"I can't sleep."

"What are you thinking about?"

Sometimes the small child would come out and say, "I was thinking that shadow looks like Thomas the Choo Choo train." But on more than one occasion the knowing child scared her daddy straight.

"God sent me here," she told him one evening. "I will never leave you."

Greg asked me if I thought there was anything *odd* about our daughter. "It's like she has magical powers," he said. I was convinced all children had magical powers.

In that first year of her becoming my daughter, I often heard of the alternate universe known as the Pink House. There was a pink Mommy and Daddy, a pink car, a pink church, and pink babies. She used to tell me as a matter of fact that she had to go to her Pink House and that she would be back for dinner. Sometimes she was going to visit her Pink Mommy and Daddy. Other times, she said that her pink babies were crying and she had to go take care of them. I always humored her.

"Well, why don't we go to the Pink House tomorrow, because I thought we would play a game after dinner?"

"Okay, Mommy, but I must go to the Pink House soon. My babies need me." I always thought that tomorrow would come and she would forget about what I said about her going to the Pink House, but she never forgot.

"But you said . . ."

"I know, honey, but that was before I knew we needed to do laundry and fold clothes today."

"Mommy, I will go by myself. You can stay here, and I will be right back." I watched her grab a sack, pack some toys and underwear and head for the door.

"Okay, but, honey, I have to go with you. It's my job to keep you safe."

"Okay, Mommy."

"Come on, JB. We're going with Jodi to the Pink House."

"We are?!" He shouted with his eyes opened wide.

"Yep," Out of the house we went. "You lead the way, honey." I stayed a couple of steps behind my three-year-old as she traversed across the lawns of our neighbors. We walked halfway down the block with Jodi leading the way. Abruptly she stopped, saying, "Mommy, I think we should go another day . . . it's kind of getting late."

Later, JB declared, "I have a blue house, you know?"

"Do you?" I asked.

"Yes . . . and in my blue house I have blue dresses I could wear whenever I want!" He was a boy often inspired by his sister's strength of will.

We played Duck, Duck, Gray Duck in the basement and laughed and laughed that day, a tired Mother Goose and two unusual ducklings.

When I returned to work, I first began to feel intensely alone. I woke by 5:00 a.m. to shower and dress. I would then wake the children and get them fed and ready for preschool. We felt lucky to obtain the last two available spots in Jodi and JB's preschool at the college where I worked, where I could drop them off and make it to my office in less than five minutes. Getting the children ready for school included packing lunch for them every day and packing their sleep sack, with a snuggly included for quality nap times.

On the first day of picking the children up, I grew quickly aware our family was unlike the other families at preschool. A parent would arrive, and a child would scream out for their parent, run to them, and thrust themselves into open arms of the waiting parent. On that very first day I arrived, I walked in to find my new children deeply involved with their play. The very moment Jodi set eyes on me she went into hysterics. "I don't want to go home! I want to stay here!"

"Don't worry," Jodi's primary teacher said to me. "Oftentimes children don't realize they get to come back tomorrow."

Tomorrow came and the same thing happened. Wednesday came, and again there was more gnashing of teeth, and I had to pick her up and carry the thirty-four-month-old crying child out to the car. JB would cooperate, though he did not appear to be too eager to go home, either. "Why do we have to leave?" he simply asked.

Each evening I explained to the twins that no one lived at school. In the evening everyone went home. The other children went home, all of the teachers went home, even the maintenance folks who they saw the last hour of the day getting the place ready for the next day. We all got to go home and be with our families. Though my children did not say it, I heard them both ask when they would get to go home with their family. I understood that even after the previous thirty days of them calling me Mommy. Mommy was a name like any other, like Sally, or Sue, or Sherrie. I was this lady who took them away from the one place they knew as home. I decided to try to act wisely, and work very hard to not let my children see I felt sad they were disappointed about going home. It was going to take time for them to know our home was their home.

In my second week back to work the loneliness I felt in the new task of raising children intensified. Motherhood was not turning out the way I thought it would. I was parenting alone. I shopped for the children. I played with them. I fed them. I bathed them. I took them to school. I brought them home. I read stories before bed, prayed with them and tucked them in at night. Greg worked late.

He was becoming a different man right in front of my very eyes. When he was at home he was distant from us, especially from me. It seemed as if he took offense of my existence. When he did talk to me, it was often to insult me in some way. When I called him from work, he never could talk. One night he crawled into bed, late as usual. I rolled over and put my hand on his shoulder.

"Greg."

"Yes."

"Did you get a second job?"

"No. When would I have the time to work a second job?!" He growled.

"I know you're worried about the finances, so I thought you might have decided to get a second job without telling me."

"Well, I wouldn't have to be so worried about the finances if you weren't such a drain. I'm getting tired of supporting you and this writing hobby. If I started living for myself for a change, you wouldn't be in this house!" He got out of bed, grabbed pillows and left the room. He slept that night in the room that doubled as an office and a TV room since the children came to live with us. I lay awake with burning eyes, agonizing over my marriage. If only I could understand what was happening to us.

The next day I went online to look for a new job. I was unhappy with the way he expressed his distaste for my modest pay at the college, but I considered that he had a point. I was content in the world of low-paying nonprofit work where the mission was one's greatest reward. I remembered my earlier vision from college that I neglected to share with him, wherein I would fight causes and he would finance them.

At work I was incredibly distracted. I needed to find a new job. My husband had become my greatest adversary, and I couldn't figure out what I needed to do to change this. I always knew before.

Whenever there was tension between us and it got to be too much, I'd make a candle-light dinner. I pulled out my prettiest clothes. Played light jazz. Dimmed lights. We all know. We've all done it, and it usually works. But nothing worked anymore. More and more I realized I could do nothing right for him. He blamed me for his lack of involvement with the children. He said I was acting as if I didn't want him to do anything. He was never around and when he was, he was breezing in and out. He stayed away from home and when he was there, he only reminded me of what a burden I was. All the while I was perplexed and wondered how I became a burden. Not long before that, he had said I was the best thing that had ever happened to him. I tried to stay awake for him at night.

The more distant and angry he grew, the more I worked, the more restrictive my diet became, the more intense my abdominal workouts became, the more I attempted to have dinner ready. He just shoveled food into his body and left night after night. Each night, I came to the table with my plate in hand as he got up from the table, dropped his dishes in the kitchen sink, and left our home.

• • •

At night after putting the children to bed, I used to make my way to my laptop and attempt to force words onto a blank screen. *On Becoming Your Mother* was the working title. Writing often felt like a selfish act in the early days of motherhood. It required a considerable amount of time and solitude, two resources mothers give up when they decide to become mothers. But we would steal time and enforce quiet in order to do what must be done. A person was only a writer if she wrote. There was the hope, at least, that in that act of selfishness her words might intersect with the life of another just in time. Choosing to believe that there was altruism in writing enhanced my desire to be a responsible "co-creator" with the Divine, as Madeline L'Engle said. I felt less self-indulgent as a writer of memoir, when I remembered what Dorothy Day said in her autobiography: "Writing a book is hard because you are giving yourself away. You write as you are impelled to write. You write about yourself because in the long run all man's [insert woman's] problems are the same, his [insert her] human need for sustenance and love." I might be giving myself away. . . . My hope was that writing was the very opposite of selfishness. What was even loftier still was what Day said next, "I can only write what I know of myself, and I pray with St. Augustine, Lord that I may know myself in order to know Thee." The better acquainted we are with ourselves, the better acquainted we are with God. In many quiet hours, I wanted this to be true.

The house at the end of Thurber Road, one block from the cemetery, was hushed, and I would be alone in that quiet house with sleeping children. It was my time to reunite with the neglected child that lingered inside of me. I opened the file of *Becoming . . .* , I'd read the last couple of paragraphs before determining where the story went from that point. The words would eventually blur in front of me. Suddenly, I'd feel as though my brain was a coil of wet potato peel. I'd make an attempt to connect with the trolls living in my subconscious mind, as John Fenn told all his students. "Let the trolls write the story. They know it better than you." But at that hour my trolls had all gone to sleep.

After ten minutes of forcing words out and poking my trolls with a pitchfork to no avail, the heaviness of my eyes had its way. I was usually too tired to turn the computer off. I climbed into bed with whatever I was wearing and that would be that. On occasion, I had the good intention of taking a short nap and waking later to write. I might set the clock for 2:00 or 3:00 in the morning. The clock shocked me awake. I jumped out of bed to hit the device, strategically placed out of reach, turned the damn thing off and slumped back into bed. Repositioning my head on my pillows, I noticed Greg's absence, cried myself awake and then pretended to be asleep when I heard his footsteps on the stairs. At that point he didn't even make it to our bedroom. I found him a few hours later, a stranger on my couch, still fully dressed, television on. I no longer felt like I was losing him. I already knew he was gone.

3

When Madison and I were girls, we lived in different regions of the country. I grew up in a housing project in Brooklyn. She grew up in a housing project in Milwaukee. Both towns were afflicted by segregation, as well as racial and economic disparities. Madison appreciated her town's summer of festivals that celebrated the variety of ethnic backgrounds, including her own. She loved television shows about black kids from struggling families who had dreams of being successful. She especially loved the sitcom that centered on students from Hillman College, the fictitious historically black college, because she had dreams of attending college. The characters in the Westerns she watched with her mother seemed to follow a particular code of honor, with a sheriff who would make things right for the residents of their town—although later she recognized how offensive those stories were in their portrayal of people of color, especially native peoples. She loved hip-hop that attempted to raise consciousness within the black psyche. She fantasized about going to Hawaii because she always wanted to experience heaven before she died. We were very aware of the impact of social constructs like race, class, and gender as black girls from low-income families. She became a sociologist to research the issues and educate others on the issues. My impatient nature did not lend itself to a life of research. I had always wanted to be a practitioner, on the ground with people who simply needed to be inspired to believe in themselves and treat others with a kindness that stemmed from inner wisdom. That was what I always needed.

For years I'd been writing things down to get them out, done and over with in order to put things to rest, the way one did with the dead or things no longer useful. For the most part, the end result was peace, or sometimes complacency in the guise of peace. Whatever it was, at that point I was done with it. I once thought the dirt of my youth was excavated and re-laid to look like the prairielands. My youth had not killed me like I thought it might. I was never pushed off the rooftop of our fourteen-story building. I didn't get it in a drive-by. The boy I slept with was just a memory and did not leave me with any ailment or child. I came out of the whole daughter-of-an-impoverished-single-mother status smelling rather like Ivory Soap. Instead of dying, I made it to thirty, then forty, then, beyond.

To commemorate turning thirty, I decided I wanted the focal point of my existence no longer to be the child I once was, but the mother I wanted to become. For the first time, I felt the aphorism from the 1970s black empowerment movement. *Perceive it, believe it, achieve it.* It became number one on my list of Top Ten Ways to Avoid Becoming a Victim of One's Life. Alas, I recognized the maternal gene had been revealed because I did have some guilt behind being able to say to my child, "The good Christian woman you call Mother did not wait for your father before doing the deed."

As the relatively stable thirty-year-old-woman I was, the shame I felt as a teenager had mostly turned into something else, something dead or no longer useful, and so I was done with it. I was beginning to know that shame was the shortest distance between a point and the psychiatric unit. I wanted to be about forward motion, carrying what I could and leaving behind whatever was just too damn heavy. So there I left it, back in Brooklyn with the rest of the crooks. I stepped out into the land of prairies and lakes as a woman, a wife, a student, a counselor, a friend. I felt myself to be an everyday black, middle class, educated woman who was suddenly seeking motherhood, and I was basking in the glow of my socially and internally constructed demographic.

It was like that scene in Spike Lee's film on Malcolm X. It was at the very end of the movie and Malcolm had been shot. I was sitting in the theater with Greg, who was then my boyfriend. I must have been twenty or twenty-one. I was just crying and crying, unable to move, I had no tissue, and I was just sniffling and carrying on. Anyway, Nelson Mandela is in a classroom of South African children and one by one these children each stand up and say in their South African dialect, "I AM Malcolm X." It was something of a battle cry, just like Spartacus. My new battle cry had become "I AM Mother." It went back to *perceive, believe, achieve*. "I will achieve motherhood for I have come on the other side of youth for some purpose and this must be the purpose."

Yet, all it took was a faint whiff or a muted sound of something smelled or heard before and there I could be again, walking slowly into my home of origin, amazed at how little had changed, feeling again its narrowness that closed in on me as I grew. I was sitting on the same couch, watching the same black-and-white television with the wire hanger sticking out of it. I was walking along the same linoleum floor, torn and taped in some spots and the edges curling away from the walls. Mice traveled in between the chipping plaster and the bend in the linoleum. They scratched about with speed and certainty of their environment. It was my first home of little frill.

I was reminded of my very first frill. My mother kept saying how fancy it was. "It looks so expensive. You didn't say it would be so fancy." The old one had outlived its usefulness. Even with it pulled down, I could not dress in my room. My new one was canary yellow, with fringes, and at the center a white woman made in a ceramic mold dangled from it like jewelry. Uncle Bobby explained how it was the best shade he carried at Fernandez Blinds and Shades. I wondered what other sort of people had shades with clay women hanging from their windows; people who lived in homes, detached houses you could walk completely around, upstairs-downstairs houses, with basements, with bars and bar stools, and wall paneling, and carpeted floors, with big windows and high ceilings, with new tubs and sinks without rust stains, and screen doors, with bikes out front left unattended, with grass, with station wagons pulling in the driveway, with mothers setting places at the table for each member of the family, with one parent at each end, with dessert afterwards and fresh lemonade or ice tea, or maybe a glass of milk. Today it would be a "window treatment" you would find in a room with a canopy bed with a sham, though I did not know words like canopy and sham, but their colors would be consistent with the colors of the blanket, and additional pillows would be thrown upon that kind of bed without ever being used, but pushed to the carpeted floor when it was time to sleep.

I liked my new shade very much. With a flick of the wrist, I could pull gently on the dangling lady, and the shade would rise all by itself and I would not have to stand on a chair to roll it up or down. My shade was my frill, my color, and my warming effect of the room lit by a sixty-watt bulb in the center of the ceiling. My shade was my uncle's gift to me. Uncle Bobby was rich in color with a full-bodied mustache, and very beautiful, like all of the Fernandez men. He was Roberto Fernandez II. His son would be the third, the one who played bass guitar, the one who was shot in the head by the rookie police officer for not putting out his cigarette in the subway station. They said my cousin had a bad day and did not want to hear another word from the white man. My uncle wished his son could have continued on at the blinds and shades shop, but after a while they only argued. The younger brother was not resistant to his father's wishes and had no schemes to grow the business, no need to teach the old dog new tricks.

Fernandez Blinds and Shades closed not long after the death of my uncle's namesake. Uncle Bobby drank. The quiet son could not help his father and began a mail order business which sold only blinds, not shades like jewelry. He carried his shop in a binder door-to-door, a solicitor showing potential customers the many colors, sizes, textures, some horizontal, some vertical. I was eighteen when my cousin started his own business. He liked my speaking voice, so it was my voice that callers heard when they wanted to place an order. Soon after, the item stuffed in a narrow cardboard box would arrive at the customer's home.

Uncle Bobby delivered his goods himself, hung them, took them back when they did not work, and come back again with one that would. His customers came back again and again to Church Street, where they knew him by name and he knew them.

So many years my shade hung in my old room, the ceramic lady long gone like the three Robertos. If I had known better, I would have saved her, and she would be with me now in my trinket box, one of the frills I've had acquired since childhood, along with mood lighting, shams, throw pillows, plants, framed art, crystal, and scented candles. These days my life is cluttered with frills, but none of them could ever give me dreams like my very first.

As an adult remembering home, the reverberations outside of my mother's first-floor apartment were all so identifiable, only a great deal more pronounced than they once appeared. I heard the three o'clock bustlings of active children just let out of school. The lobby carried their noise like an amplifying tunnel. I heard Jay from 111 who sold the *Daily News* each Sunday morning, floor by floor until he reached fourteen. He'd sing "Neeeews Paaaaper!" The echo reached my mother's door, and she'd scurry for change and a tip. "What a nice boy," she'd say, pulling out the coupon pages as I dug through for the TV guide. Mrs. Dockery would come knocking eventually to give us a pan of her apple stuffing. Jehovah's Witnesses would come knocking with the latest issue of *Watchtower*.

Outside, traffic moved west toward the Brooklyn Queens expressway or east toward the Brooklyn Navy Yard. Bridges and highways, vast government-subsidized buildings, city parks with graffiti-adorned handball courts. It was a landscape of infrastructure and the uninterrupted presence of people, pushing or pedaling, sitting on benches in contemplation or conversation. Sands Street craved its inhabitants the way mountains and prairies craved theirs, whatever theirs might be, bears or butterflies.

Some faces had changed, but mostly they were the same. But what was the thing that was strangely unfamiliar? I knew it was I. I was not who I thought I would be, and to some degree I found myself in the sad reflection of a misplaced dream. I always had an affinity for black women with dreadlocks, big jewelry, and something acutely honest to say. But what I was begrudged to admit at thirty was that I never became what I revered. I never locked my hair and for years I had not been unequivocally honest. What I had become was tempered. Tempered by the Midwest, tempered by marriage, by age, by middle-classdom, by religiosity, and my longings for small houses and station wagons.

I was not even sure if I could call the newer place I lived "home." I grew up with cement, not wildness. There I was living with formless raspberry bushes, which I did not pick and which I could not destroy, no matter how determined I got. I lived with rhubarb transplanted from someone's country garden. I knew nothing of these matters. I planted day lilies in the shade instead of in full sun. I dropped grass seed on a patch of dirt without watering and wondered why the grass didn't grow. I could not distinguish marigolds from carnations. I was afraid of bunnies. In good weather I went out for duty's sake, not love. Attempted to make things pretty. Failed. Greg threatened to pave the backyard.

I had the audacity to ask my slave ancestors who worked the earth without pay to help me find my agricultural roots. That helped me as much as asking my dead grandfather to help me earn an A in intermediate Spanish. I wondered why we didn't buy that townhouse instead, and then I remembered. We bought the house for outdoor birthday parties, for carrying pitchers of punch to a picnic table after Little League, for playing tag around the big oak tree that hindered the afternoon sun. We bought that house for the same reason we bought my blue station wagon. Why else would anyone buy a station wagon, blue or otherwise? Pulling out of the driveway I looked back for safety's sake, sometimes noticing the emptiness of the vehicle, and what felt like a spasm pulled at my chest, and I remembered I was a person in deep longing. Dreams had gotten me this far, far away from my home of origin. Why not dream some more, however it may twinge? Pain had its reasons for being.

In youth, I dreamt of cobblestone blocks lined with old trees and three-story brownstones with black iron railings and arched and ornate doors, with one button to push with my name next to it and an intercom for me to holler, "Come on up!" I dreamt of living close enough to my home of origin to conduct Saturday morning arts and crafts at the Farragut Projects Community Center.

My daydreams escaped Sands Street, though my night dreams still hovered there. Dreams of my deceased brother, Vernon, always took place there. I had one recurring dream in which I knocked on my mother's apartment door. Vernon answered, opened the door wide and said, "Where have you been?" I just stood there and wondered if I'd been mistaken about everything, the wheelchair, the hospitalizations, the morphine, the weight lost, the height lost, the life lost, the cremation, the ashes sitting in Daddy's apartment? I pondered his question, "Where have you been?" I had no answers because I didn't know where I had been or where I belonged.

Other dreams occurred there, dreams of me holding babies. I had my first baby dream when I was sixteen. I gave birth to a baby that looked more like a velvety red hair bow. As a thirty-year-old, I dreamt of real screaming babies, flaring tonsils at me, demanding to be fed. I dreamt of my earliest love. He and I were too young to know when the affair ended. It ended with summer, like many good things did. It ended with the fall chill that crept in quietly late in August. I stood two inches taller than he, though he was two years my senior and already in second grade. I once thought he was as permanent as the Brooklyn Queens Expressway. When I returned home for winter break from college and found him still standing or sitting on Sands Street, often with a forty-ounce bottle of malt liquor wrapped in a brown paper bag, we would always be sincerely kind to one another. "How are you, Travis?" I'd ask, and he'd say, "Well, you know, livin' livin'." I noticed how I never stopped growing long enough for him to catch up to my height and how I still loved him. I loved him like summer.

He was my brother's best friend, and together they were Kyle and Travis, small but dominant point guards on the courts on High Street, with mutual affection like Magic and Isaiah, who kissed each other's cheeks before games. But Kyle never kissed Travis. I did. It happened the day I told him he was my boyfriend and he said okay. I was five, but the memory survives and is stored where first memories are kept, in the illusory bones and muscle tissue of the soul.

I dreamt that Kyle, Travis and I were together again. We sat in my mother's living room, furnished with the same navy couches, then covered with navy slipcovers. Outside my mother's window were beautiful gardens with orange, yellow, and purple, billowing against the clouds.

"Great job on the garden," Travis said to me. I was unaware at first, but soon realized the garden was my doing.

"It still needs work," I responded with false modesty. Inside, I was lit like a firefly. We drifted in the color and I imagined myself a lilac bush swaying rhythmically at the will of the forgiving breeze. All that botanical life astounded us and it was right there in the center of our projects, just outside my mother's first floor apartment, amidst the rumble of the B37 bus thumping over steel planks that covered the potholes on Sands Street. I could have not been more satisfied. Kyle gave us peanuts, and we ate with joy and laughed just like we did during hot months, undisturbed by things to do. The night dream merged my worlds, and in this new creation I knew how to garden. I awoke from my dream and cried for the first time after learning Travis had died. Kyle said it was his liver.

Often I wished my arms had carried more of Brooklyn to the midland. I used to think I would be like the visitors I knew as a child. They returned to their home of origin with mustached husbands and fat babies. They dressed in trench coats and pumps, looking like somebody's black girl-Friday.

"Where you been?" One of the elder women would ask.

"Oh, I moved to Queens, or Virginia, or I'm stationed in Germany." They had grand white smiles, enhanced by true red lips.

I gazed at them as they passed by and greeted me by my older sister's name. I corrected them, and they said, "Girl, you got big. How old are you now?" I said seven or such and they said, "Boy, how time flies."

I never became one of the women who came back. Those who moved on, kept moving. We didn't come back to pat the children on the head saying, "My, have you grown." We were suspicious of the children. We didn't mess the coat of puppies and old tired dogs too stubborn to pass on. The pups and the old dogs had jaws that locked and were perfectly capable of removing one's hand from one's body. Instead, we sneaked in inconspicuously to visit aging mothers and darted out toward planes, trains, or automobiles and fled the disaster our home of origin had become.

In that house on Thurber, I often wondered how I come to a sense of homelessness and not knowing where to land full flesh to the ground. When I watched Greg rake the previous fall's remaining leaves, I was struck by the lack of people in the street. The few I saw were busy with the upkeep of their own personal patches of green—trimming, mowing, planting in diligent attempt to have the land submit to human wills. They didn't know that I was watching, or did not care. Surveying our own patch of green I always noticed those daylilies were struggling to grow, again in a location not meant for them. I always said that, when I got the inclination, I would move them out of the shade and replant them in full sun where they belonged.

4

MADISON MET ME near the exit of the administration building for lunch that Friday, a brief release from my sentence of coordinating meetings and keeping the gate of the chief so minor aggravations did not interrupt his highest priorities. In the days immediately following our lunch, I dwelled heavily in my imagination. Since the J-twins arrived four years before that time, Greg and I continued our arrangement. He kept his eye on the little ones on Saturday mornings. Childcare responsibilities shifted to me by the afternoon. Saturday mornings were designated writing time for me. If I could not write, I read. The Saturday morning after meeting Madison for lunch, I sat in my usual spot at the bookstore chain and ordered my habitual frosty caffeinated drink. I opened the novel I found in the Gay and Lesbian section of the store, feeling a need to educate myself on the subject of women who loved women. The sex was less than captivating. I never liked trash novels and lesbian lovers did not make them any more interesting. After leaving the store disappointed, I reread the memoir of my former writing professor about her life with her female spouse. I appreciated the book before, when I thought I was destined to live the rest of my life in heterosexuality, but it meant something more to me after meeting Madison. Her book grounded me in the reality of what life with another woman might be like. I could be happy loving a woman who loved me. Nothing about that vision seemed strange at all. Years ago I had been so afraid of the thought, and there I was so distant from the earlier fear that kept me straight all of those years. What my professor and her spouse had was the life of my dreams. Of course, we were different people, with different circumstances and different backgrounds. Of course, I would be bringing children into a brand new relationship. How would that work? And I had a marriage that still needed undoing. Is there ever really a honeymoon period when the circumstances are complicated? Those thoughts did not cross my mind at that time.

I was ready to tell someone about my infatuation. I called a writer friend who was a cohort member of mine in a twelve-week writing workshop I had recently finished. He was a gay man who had been with his husband for decades. Because he was a minister, I thought it might not have been unusual for him to receive a call out of nowhere from someone who needed to share her latest epiphany with another living soul. I was delighted and terrified when I heard his voice. I wanted someone to help me define what my connection to Madison meant, but I knew if I asked this out loud, I would never be able to take it back.

Madison was not the first woman to occupy my internal space. To my recollection, it started at thirteen when I was too soft to go to school with those crazy-ass giants. The two housing projects were just blocks away from each other which, of course, meant a long-time rivalry between the two developments. The belief among Farragut youth was that Fort Green produced giants that could easily devour us whenever they felt ready. Farragut kept them sleeping by staying the hell off their turf and being cautious when we knew Fort Green was on our ground.

During the summer of 1983, my classmate, Freeman Johnson, the born leader with the deep dimples and wavy hair who never ever spoke to me for any reason whatsoever, along with members of his crew, agreed I was just too soft for McKinney Junior High. They felt I would be the first among them to fall. This unexpected conversation happened the day I was kicking the city dust with Gwen as we strolled through the neighborhood with nothing to do. Gwen was one of my best friends and was considered "fly" by most of the neighborhood. She was prone to acute superficiality, but for some reason, Gwen still felt the need to have at least one authentic friendship. I was selected to fill this need. I will always love Gwen for being my first reader. She was the only living person to read all one hundred and twenty-nine pages of my first manuscript, written with my blue electric typewriter.

"So, what school ya'll goin' to in the fall?" Freeman asked.

"McKinney," Gwen and I both answered. A limited number of kids in the neighborhood were able to avoid the fate of McKinney by enrolling in P.S. 8, the middle school in the closest white neighborhood. Freeman assumed me I would be one of those kids trying to escape. Freeman shook his head and spoke directly to me for the first time in the six years we'd been classmates. Very seriously and with some measure of concern, he said, "You're going to die. You're too soft."

I considered myself duly warned on Farragut Day. The annual celebration was a day-long neighborhood block party in which the streets that ran between three blocks of fourteen-story buildings would be closed off. The young ones would spend the day rocketing down the long smooth tar on roller skates. As the sun went down, DJs began setting up equipment for the long-awaited evening jam. Grand Master and Melly-Mel's White Lines hit the wheels of steel, and there was a collective, "Owww." Was anyone enraptured by the anti-drug message in the lyrics, as bodies began to simultaneously undulate with the insistent bass that carried the message? Arms in the air, waving like we just didn't care. Girls started doing the weblo. Even I felt the rhythm of that magnificent July night and rocked my curve-less body in sync with the crowd. It was our day of celebration. Bellies were full of grilled hotdogs and artificially flavored grape or orange soda. Psyches were caught up in the music. Our music had been birthed on streets just like the one they were dancing on that night, the street where the boys played *skellies* and the girls jumped Double Dutch. This was a time before NWA, before east versus west coast, before the word "gangsta" became constituted in black urban vernacular. All was not yet lost.

Yet I had an acute awareness of danger. I noticed those unfamiliar guys lurking on the periphery of the crowd, not participating, not dancing, not scanning the crowd of dancing girls in search of the one with the finest body. Instead of waving in the air, their arms were folded across their chests as if they were bouncers. But this was not a nightclub. This was our neighborhood. The looks on their faces said that they were holding a secret that would soon be shared with everyone. I did not want to stay to find out. I tried to alert Gwen. "These guys don't seem right," I whispered. Gwen ignored me and continued dancing (with the boy who would end up fathering her son three years later). People often ignored me when I tried to clue them into danger. It was just like the time when I tried to warn Natasha, my best friend, that "Stink-Abe" was about to sic his dog, Whitey, on us. I could feel that boy's repressed rage on my skin from several feet away though he acted as if the name-calling didn't bother him none. I knew better than to go near him or his nasty albino dog that was off his leash and trotting in the distance. Just like the day when Whitey chased my friends and chomped down on the back of Natasha's leg, I knew it was time to leave because I knew those guys at the jam were no damn good. I could feel it in my body. Just like the old people with bad bones could feel rain coming, I could feel hate that produced the ugliest of storms. I followed my instincts and hurried down Sands Street to my building, which was unusually desolate for a Saturday night. Folks were either down the street at the jam or already in their apartments. I sighed hard with relief when Ma answered the door right away. My mother normally would have been asleep at that time, but she couldn't sleep while her youngest child, who preferred the indoors, was still outdoors in the late evening. Ma locked the door behind her and went to bed. I sat by the open window in our living room, still feeling the consoling breeze against my arm and cheek and still bouncing my head to the early '80s rap that blasted throughout the neighborhood. Was I just being the chicken-shit I was known for being? I thought that was probably the case until I heard the first *pop, pop, pop* of the shots being fired, then screams. I ducked and crawled to my room and stayed on the floor until all of Farragut went silent. Gwen told me the next day it was some dudes from Fort Green, not to my surprise. Before the shots were fired, one of them shouted, "Fort Green in the House!" It seemed as if their mission was not to maim, but to end Farragut Day on their terms with a bang.

•••

That was the summer just before McKinney. I wasn't sure how my sense for danger was going to protect me while in school. I couldn't just leave when I wanted. Freeman was right. I was too soft, and plain, and goober-like. How was I just going to arrive at school in octagon glasses straight from the welfare rack? I needed to change my image so I wouldn't show up on my first day looking like a bona fide sucker. I knew well-dressed kids and good-looking kids were less likely to be targets. I had to find a way to appease the gods of Fort Green.

I called Daddy and explained why I could not go to junior high wearing welfare glasses. Instead of lecturing me, he indulged me. Daddy took me to buy a new pair of glasses for forty-two dollars. For the first time in my life, I owned eyewear that wasn't paid for by the government. We found a pair of large red Pierre Cardin's, just like the kind Sally Jesse Rafael wore. My friends liked them so much they asked if they could borrow them just to be fashionable. My older brother, who was twenty-five years old and working at the New York Stock Exchange, treated me to a week's worth of new outfits that made me feel as cute as Tootie from *Facts of Life*. My favorite ensemble was the black pinstripe pants that were wide at the hip and tapered at the ankle and a silky white blouse with ruffles and puffy sleeves. I loved the patent-leather shoes that would later be stolen right off my feet by some grown women who claimed to have just been released from Riker's Island State Penitentiary. I wasn't as fast as my brother Kyle, who ran home when Fort Green was on the heels of his brand new sneakers that he purchased with his summer job money. I remembered the day Vince and Travis knocked frantically on our apartment door to tell my mother Kyle was being chased by Fort Green. They'd already waved down a patrol car waiting outside for Ma to come out and help with the search. I climbed in after her. My eyes darted from corner to corner in search of the brother I couldn't imagine being without. I'd heard stories of guys being killed for their jackets or shoes. Ma and I rejoiced when we learned Kyle beat us home with his leather sneakers still on his feet.

When I was confronted with the same decision to run, to fight, or to hand over my shoes, I chose the path of least resistance and felt some relief in the fact I was wearing thick socks, too thick, really, to wear with those shiny black dress shoes, but thick enough to keep my feet warm on my cold and humiliating walk home.

• • •

Most of the time, I knew how to pay attention and notice when trouble was about to happen. Of course, there were times when it was harder to get away. There was Mark Hayes, who hurled basketballs at me in gym class, and the two boys who body slammed me in the snow, but they were mostly boys who had felt unwanted urges toward me, the uncool chick, and didn't know how to express them. Luckily, Mark had bad aim and the snow was sympathetic.

I regrouped after exhausting days of defensive living in a girl's body. Being a girl might mean having my behind groped on the lunch line and looking behind me to find a pile of trifling boys grinning in my face. No one wanted to take the blame, but no one gave up his friend, either. My tears ignored my warnings and dropped anyway. Another day, being a girl might mean having a foot land on my ass and being shoved to the ground because I did not respond to some boy's rap. On the worst day, being a girl meant nearing the entrance of our school building and being asked by an older boy, too old for junior high, with a scratchy matchbox voice and lifeless eyes, how much would I charge for a blow job. Though I did not know what that meant, I noticed my hands shaking. I was afraid. I believe this was near the time when the dreams of the girl with the gentle ways began. In my dreams, I touched another girl's hair.

Some days, even while awake, I was relieved to be a girl. I came through my first year of junior high without any visible bruises. I thought of Freeman Johnson's warning the day I was leaving school and noticed a small crowd of kids in the street, preventing traffic from passing. I could tell it was a fight when I heard a boy from Fort Green shout, "Beat that motherfucker down!" I walked slowly past the crowd that was starting to grow, and I could see Freeman Johnson's face. He lay on the ground in the fetal position as a foot came down on his head over and over.

No one tried to stop the fight. No one went back to the school for help. I continued walking, clutching my books all the way home.

Freeman was a boy who was prettier than most girls and certainly better dressed. But he offered Fort Green nothing but a challenge for their women, which meant, of course, that he needed to be destroyed. But destruction only begot destruction as Freeman changed from the destroyed to the destroyer. It took one armed robbery and one dead girl to change his status.

There were some collisions between the world of my imagination and the world I walked through in real time. Soon, there wasn't much distinction between the kids I knew from Farragut and the ones I heard about from Fort Green. The streets became about making money. A young man from Farragut could kill his neighbor and childhood friend if he thought it was necessary. Many of us wondered what happened. Where did we go wrong? Some blamed the white man who supplied the drugs. Some blamed joblessness and limited opportunities for our young men. Some blamed the previous generation for failing to educate the youth about the cultural traditions of black and brown peoples. The church folks said nobody but the devil himself could tear a community down as thoroughly and completely as we had been torn down. As a child, I had no idea who to blame. As occasional gunfire turned nightly, I only knew it was more than I could stand.

In my dreams, I touched the girl's hair—thick and always parted down the middle and partially shoved into tiny rubber bands. Anita managed to survive by staying unnoticed, but I noticed her. I noticed her every day. I was attracted to her kindness and wondered how she could remain so copasetic while growing up in the land of giants.

I found myself sitting next to Anita on the school bus that transported us during one particular field trip. I was delighted to find alone time with the girl who entered my dreams. Anita was even more soft-spoken than I, but she smiled easily . . . openly. Life presented me with an opportunity to make a connection, and I was more scared than grateful. Friendships often start with a compliment, so I searched my mind for one that would be sincere and somehow express my admiration of Anita.

"You're an average student," is what came out and as soon as it did, I wished could snatch the words with my hand and crush them into dust. "I mean . . . that's not what I meant to say." I quickly tried to correct myself. "You're an *above*-average student," I said, realizing this wasn't much better and did not nearly get to the heart of my deep fondness for this girl.

"You're right. I am an average student," Anita said, remaining gracious and humble, as always. "You're the one who is an above-average student."

"I'm an A student," I said to be more precise. Anita only gave a half-smile and turned to look out the window. For many days after, I tortured myself by reliving that moment with Anita. I didn't realize I was so proficient in speaking jackass, but that's exactly what I spoke every time I was near her. But the simple truth was that this fascination with Anita could not possibly go anywhere, anyway. Being a girl meant being limited to boys who kicked, and groped, and hurled objects at you at top speed.

Soon, my status changed too. The following year, I did not get a new wardrobe and my Sally Jesse glasses had to be held together by Scotch tape. Fort Green boys like Douglass and Mark stopped noticing me. On the rare occasion they did, the boys appeared confused, sometimes disgusted. I imagined they were wondering what they ever saw in me. But I was fine with that. I became less and less a target and was soon welcomed into the realm of glorious invisibility where I learned they didn't kick me if they didn't see me.

Still, I longed to run away from the violence of the projects. I wanted relief. I needed to feel safe, at least some of the time. I asked Daddy if I could live with him, my stepmother, and little sister. I never asked before. I always assumed it wouldn't be up for discussion. I was surprised when he said yes. I was even more surprised my mother let me go.

In my early years, I was lost without my mother and could not bear being away from her for too long. That was how I ended up on the stoop of my father and stepmother's apartment building in Clinton Hill, a neighborhood to a professional black community including Wall Street employees, teachers, and politicians. That was how I ended up being within kissing distance of a boy who was too old for me, although I didn't know it at first.

I was a girl inhaling New York City's pollutants, almost believing that if I tried hard enough, I could be like Francie Nolan's tree that grew rough and regal right out of the concrete. I read and reread *A Tree Grows in Brooklyn* that summer, which left me feeling ripe for my first teenage summer romance. However, I did question whether or not I could actually consider myself a teenager. Teenagers went to high school and worked at fast food restaurants. Teenagers got learner's permits and went on dates to the movies without adult supervision. I was too young to do any of those things. Thirteen is a bizarre age to be a girl. The mind is a lump of formless dough waiting to be shaped into something useful to society. Although the body is in its most glorious state, we are too clueless to know it. My long legs would never be as lean. In a short span of time, I would lose my ability to run for miles without losing my breath. I didn't know that time would be so brief. I thought I would go on that way forever.

I wondered if I was the weird girl from someplace else in the minds of the other young people in the neighborhood, who never inquired. I spent most of my days with my primary companion, my five-year-old sister—the creation of Daddy's second marriage. I enjoyed tranquility while pushing the happy girl on a swing at the park or holding her hand as she learned to roller-skate. The smallest things would make her light up, and my time with her had its rewards. My presence seemed to go unnoticed by the adolescents in the neighborhood, who all congregated on the same stoop at some point in the day or evening. I was not at home, and I was lonely for peer interaction like what I enjoyed in the projects.

Ryan was an exquisitely crisp boy who wore white whites and bright brights, never dingy or faded. His dark hair sparkled in midday and glistened from afro-sheen. By one gaze, he could lift me off the stoop of that brownstone apartment building and welcome me into the world of black bourgeoisie. I spent hours on the stoop, reading or scribbling random thoughts in my journal. When he walked past our brownstone, he was bold enough to give me a deep stare that did not cause me to want to hide or run away. We did not speak. I watched him watch me, and started timing his stroll from the other end of the block around the dinner hour. I wasn't sure how he was spending his summer days, but he kept a regular schedule. I hated the feeling of invisibility, and it was a relief to know someone other than my family could see me.

"Hello," he finally spoke.

"That wasn't so hard now, was it?" My stepmother said and promptly got up and went inside. She had something to do with him saying hello. She put him up to it. I could not get anything out beyond a breathless hello.

"That's your aunt, right?"

"My stepmother."

He wanted to know where I came from, a question I wanted someone to ask me for some reason. I would have said Farragut. It was still my home and the place where my mother and siblings still lived, though I was trying to mold myself into the type of girl who would live in Clinton Hill, a black girl with middle class parents who would read on the stoop, sketch the tree in front of her brownstone, and envision a placid life.

"Do you play backgammon?" he asked.

"I never played before."

"I can teach you sometime."

"Okay."

"Will you be here tomorrow?" Which was kind of a silly question given that I had been waiting for him in the same spot every evening.

"Yes."

"I'll come by tomorrow night, then."

"Okay," I said.

During the day, I imagined myself as some man's wife. I was going to be a schoolteacher married to a businessman who wore tailored suits and carried a briefcase, like my brother who worked at the stock exchange. My daydreams did not match my night dreams. While asleep, I dreamt about modest Anita, even more modest than I. In my night dreams, she and I were carefree and blameless youth who held each other's faces and smiled at one another. While awake, I was ashamed and embarrassed by thoughts of finding comfort with another girl. While awake, I chose to imagine my life with a boy who would become a man. I would live a normal life, approved by others. I would be a girl from the inner city who grew up to live an admirable life like folks featured in *Ebony Magazine*. There was something very wrong with liking another girl that way, just as there was something wrong with drinking, smoking, not doing homework, and not believing in God. Good girls, safe girls married boys with well-shaped 'fros—and raised children who would take piano lessons and travel abroad with hopes of elevating themselves, their entire families, and their entire communities to new heights. This was what we all wanted. Every American. Or, so I had assumed.

5

After meeting Madison for lunch that particular workday, the need for men and the approval of others turned to ashes. With Madison, need blended with want so thoroughly I could not distinguish one from the other until all I felt was bliss about the possibility of a new life.

Before coming to work for the numero uno vice president and meeting Madison, when I was in between universities and temping for a living, I acknowledged my feelings for a painter and a writer who also landed in temp work. She loved Nina Simone. She adorned her legs with the work of her favorite tattoo artist and had fusion hair—Amy Brenneman meets Tracee Ellis Ross. We brought our gym shoes to work and power-walked to the nearest park. We talked about our artistic projects. After I stopped temping and went to work at the Catholic university, I purposely drifted away when the dreams of my walking companion began. She loved her husband and described him as a good-hearted person. I wanted a "good-hearted" person of my own. My marriage was no longer tied to its roots, but I was still married.

After meeting Madison for lunch, I wondered more about my journey. Madison had always been so clear about what she wanted and what she needed to do in order to get there. I wondered how I spent so many years of my life confused, although I had claimed many times to be self-aware.

I've tried very hard to penetrate the skin of the eighteen-year-old I was when I met Greg. I held my disappointments in my abdomen just beneath my diaphragm, the way I still do. I rose three days a week for Intro to Psych, which met in Monroe Lecture Hall at 7:50 a.m., always with two cornrows in my hair, always with my right shoe worn more than the left and slightly leaning, always in the same black utilitarian three-quarter length coat, always with no gloves or hat, always with jeans slightly above my ankles, tight around my middle, and thinning at the knees, always wearing an ill-fitted bra, and wide-rim glasses that slid to the tip of my nose. I was the one who often fell asleep in morning classes, who often passed gas in my sleep according to the classmates who whispered and giggled behind me. Perhaps that is how I kept going, passing all of my disappointments held in my abdomen right out of my ass and into the faces of those who mocked me.

Some understood this was our time to be young. The dorms cleared out on Friday nights. The white students would overcrowd the local bars and black students would be "bumpin'" at an AKA party. I couldn't take all that house music. That loud techno-shit only served to shock my eardrums. By that time, I preferred quiet, acoustic, and deliciously sad.

Greg Carter had a word for sisters like me, "Brewster Women." It was a code phrase to mean a sister who acted as if she did not appear to care for guys. Or, sisters who did not put forth much effort in having guys notice her. I knew I was a bit of a mess and out of step with my peers. There were people like Tommy Waters. I was subject to his judgment of me. To him, I was undesirable. "Ugly" was the actual word used. It was hard to understand why I internalized the insults of a malnourished ratfish, no matter how well dressed he was or how many gold chains he could hang from his bony neck.

During some stages in my life I forced myself to care, and my classmates did recognize this. "Who's that pretty girl sitting with Greg Carter?" one boy asked another. They were embarrassed to realize it was me, the "ugly girl" who had done something with her hair and painted her lips. I couldn't keep it up. I had other priorities. The quest for popularity seemed incredibly absurd by the time I arrived at college. Higher education was going to be my passageway to a purposeful life.

I relished my weekend solitude when most people left campus to spend time at home, including Greg Carter. On Sundays, I hid for hours in the library before the weekend home dwellers returned that evening to pile into the dining centers or the common areas of the dormitories. Alone, I inhaled my final moments of peace and read Audre Lorde. "I dream of a place between your breasts to build my house like a haven." I had similar dreams as Audre, but also knew that nothing could come of it. I indulged my interest in womanly tenderness in secret places of the eleven-story library. I had little desire to become one of the members of Lambda Nu, the co-ed GLBT fraternity that displayed their homosexuality in everyone's gawking distance. I felt crazy enough and as much as I found myself on the periphery of black student life, I wasn't ready for them to pry my already tattered black card completely from my hands.

There were other ways to explore this identity without joining a club, without claiming it as an identity. Everyone knew of those stunning black brothers teetering between two worlds. They made headlines with their masterful performance of *The Vogue* at the annual talent show sponsored by the Black Student

Union. They were gorgeous, confident and didn't give a shit about what anyone said about them. People could think whatever they wanted. But if they were asked, they would simply say it was nobody's damn business. They were an exclusive society that took special authorization to penetrate. I was envious of their friendship and the fact that no matter what the other students on campus said about them, they always had each other.

Who did I have? The other girls in Lambda were white, middle class, intellectual and liberated. I was still bound by invisible chains just like the afrocentric clinical psychologist spoke of when he came to campus. I was enthralled by Na'im Akbar. Unfortunately, I did not recognize myself as one who needed to break free from historical bondage. I thought I was free because I was a college student. I was on the path to upward mobility, so I thought. We all were. We'd made it to college. Everything would fall into place for all of us.

I did not know any female students of color who gave the appearance of being interested in women. New York was the territory of ethnic ghettos, where everyone stuck with their own kind. Black students only pledged black fraternities and sororities. It was not common for people to date outside their group. The one exception might have been the one or two star athletes who were allowed into the white universe, and thus expelled themselves from the black life entirely. It was the way it was in the 1980s. You had to pick a side. No one at that Long Island school was free to do whatever the hell they wanted without paying a price. It is possible I could have imagined all this, but I believed there were codes to follow. I still asked myself the question, "What would people think of me?" In all of my youth, I remained low on the social scale. I was afraid of dropping into the abyss. In my internal life, I was a girl who preferred to do my own thing, and I was desperate to have the personal space to figure out just what my own thing was. If it was loving women, I was never going to find out in that environment. The black women I knew were either seriously into guys or seriously into God.

In all of my social awkwardness, I wasn't shy about sharing my affinity for black women with heart and something acutely honest to say. I gave teary defenses of Alice Walker's right to tell the stories she needed to tell. I was the self-proclaimed number one fan of Tracy Chapman, who gave me permission to love folk music out loud and in public. Very loud and completely off-key, I sang all of Tracy's lyrics. I believed the song about the rootless young woman who stopped trying to be what others expected her to be was written for me. Like Tracy, I knew I was connected to my people even if my people didn't always embrace me as one of their own. I believed my life was supposed to matter for some greater good. I wasn't exactly sure what form it would take. I hoped I could be brave enough to work in a neighborhood like the one where I grew up. Perhaps I would teach children, or start a nonprofit to encourage teenage girls. I lived most of my present in the future, so that the present only mattered in how it would get me to realize the future. I felt there was so much to learn and, for me, most of that learning needed to be done in solitude. Still, I did recognize that I was part of a community of shared history and plight. I felt like the other black students on the Long Island campus, urbanites living after Yussef Hawkins had died, when Gavin Kato and Yankel Rosenbaum were still alive, and the street wars of Crown Heights hadn't yet erupted. It was the year Jesse ran for president for the second time. A bunch of us sat together that summer to listen to his "Keep Hope Alive" speech at the DNC. I could not say for sure I knew what hope felt like at eighteen with undercurrents of disappointment and madness traveling in my bowels.

I read and re-read Asata Shakur's poem that commanded the young to carry on the resistance. Victimization was for the weak and needy, and I was trying to be neither. It was easy to feel brave when I didn't leave my dorm room on Friday nights in order to write sloppy poetry with dull pencils. My only companions were the photo of my girl, Tracy Chapman, that I cut out from an issue of *Rolling Stone* magazine, and the photo of Antonio who made me make a promise.

I found Antonio in *Essence* magazine. He was a broad-shouldered child at twelve, wearing a simple white T-shirt, his hair cut into a flat top. Underneath his photo were the words, "Can I be your son?" I made that promise to this boy, who could have been a paid model for all I knew, that someday I would take in a boy like him and be his mother and love away his sorrows over all he'd lost and all that he'd never had. I was eighteen and still shocked I made it to college alive and almost in one piece. But I was sincere in my promise. I thought that perhaps that might be my great purpose in life, to mother motherless children and raise them to be original thinkers with more courage than I possessed.

• • •

At that time I met Greg. It took time for me to start feeling those sorts of feelings that kind of, sort of felt like love. It wasn't like he came out of nowhere. We all come from somewhere, and he came from Brooklyn, just like I did. By the time he came, I was ready to let something else in other than the words of the iconic women I admired. We went on our first date at the end of my first year. It was a week before my nineteenth birthday, a week before I would be gone for the rest of the summer to serve as a peer counselor for the incoming students of color in "the program." When we were apart, he wrote me letters. There was one card with a picture of a calendar, and he scribbled a note about him counting the days before he would see me again.

A couple of older female students in the program cautioned me against Greg. Dana, a senior, dated the president of the black student union and one of the most respected brothers in black society on campus. She was a down sister—earthy, proud and confident enough to wear a natural cut close to her head while most of the black girls were straightening their hair. By that time, I gave in and was making regularly visits to the salon for "touch-ups." Dana was the sister who introduced me to Asata and did her best to educate younger women on the contributions of black women who fought for our freedom just as hard as any man. I admired Dana's strength and hoped to emulate her prowess someday. However, it wasn't going to happen that summer as a rising sophomore.

Things with Greg began gradually after the start of my second year. I sat in my oversized denim shirt and oversized socks. My hair would be out and as wild as it wanted to be. I was going to become a teacher of children like the child I had been and preach Kujichagaulia, self-determination, tapping the imagination to exist mentally beyond their physical circumstances. It was how I made it to college.

Greg wanted badly to be a corporate brother. He was a *Wall Street* reading, stock market playing business major. I wanted to fight causes, and he said he would finance them.

Before this, I was never one to go visit my family on weekends and holidays. But during the Christmas of 1989, I saw a glimpse of my future. I wanted to consider a future full of ordinary. I was terrified of meeting his family and asked if he would come to my rescue when I needed him. I'd let him know when I needed him by scratching my chin. The front door crept open, and I was met by a man holding a video camera. "Well, who do we have here? It's my nephew, Gregory, and his new girlfriend." Greg introduced me to the cameraman who felt the footage was too good not to keep it rolling. I stepped behind my new boyfriend and followed him into the foyer. Someone took my coat. I smiled and tried to be polite. There were more uncles and aunts, and cousins, and wives of cousins, and neighbors, a brother, a longtime girlfriend of the brother, a sister, and a new boyfriend of the sister. There were the college friends of the brother's girlfriend. There was a Godmother and two Godsisters. Lastly, there was a mother and a father who had invited all of these people to their house for Christmas. This was going to be one of many gatherings I would spend with these people who took me in like a lost child looking for a home. At the end of those visits, his mother would always send me on my way with a giant helping of Georgian leftovers and a big squeeze. "We sure enjoyed you, Sherrie," she always said. I would come to love her dearly as she became part mother, part friend, and part teacher as she taught me her style of cooking, though I could never quite duplicate her unwritten recipes.

• • •

For me, it wasn't all of a sudden. It was more like I was a well, being filled by a thimble. I didn't even recognize the trickles of warm, soothing, sweet-smelling oils being consistently dropped into me. I awoke one morning, and I was completely saturated until it leaked out of my pores. Soon I couldn't touch anything without leaving traces of my fullness behind. Was this fullness love? Love is a word with no love in it. I believed that.

Still, I felt like that little Irish Francie Nolan's tree towering above all that threatened me. Although, I was vulnerable to another human being—not just a human being but also a man, and not just a man, but also a twenty-year-old. Trusting my heart to a young man was an extreme sport. The potential for breakage was predictably high. But as a young woman, I was unaware of the danger. I assumed they were like me, happy for love, mystified, not petrified.

He did not interrupt. He never appeared apathetic. He called me Ms. Williams and when he came to visit, he always called first. "Ms. Williams, I was thinking about coming over to see you." When he arrived at my room, he said, "Good evening, Ms. Williams. How are you?" For a while, I forgot he was nineteen with his tied shoes and muted colors while celebrity homeboys wore neon. During the birth of hip-hop sprawling into mainstream, my new boyfriend was wearing the sweaters purchased for him by his mother. *They come this way?* I wondered. I was attracted to the understatement that caused me to believe there was something deeper happening beneath the gray that covered his brown body.

The other guys called him "Professor" because he was good in math and helped them from time to time. He was a junior, a finance major who looked after the black and brown freshmen, calling each of us by our last names. The Latino posse would hang in his room as if it was the neighborhood community center built to keep disadvantaged youth off the street, providing guidance to Mr. Hernandez, Mr. Rosaro, Mr. Lora, and the tall skinny one who always knocked his knees together in his chair whenever he laughed—Ernesto Something. It was too late for Mr. Rosaro, because he had already gotten his girlfriend pregnant the summer before school would start.

But Mr. Carter reserved judgment, found himself a mentor to the multicultural students, although we were still called minorities, the good, the nasty, the nerdy, the beautiful, the popular, the unaware, and the freak who quickly became his girlfriend . . . then, slowly, became his wife.

• • •

I am like my own head of damaged hair
Being rampaged by split ends in desperate need of trimming
In need of replenishment like
My dying skin

• • •

We married on Jeroloman Street at the Brooklyn Court House. I wore a silver dress. Only his parents attended us, and we would live with them for the first seven months of our marriage before skipping town, leaving Boot-Hill as if our very lives depended on it. I wanted a town that slept a silent, deep, rested kind of sleep. And that is how we ended up across the street from the cornfields in a town called Eagan, a Saint Paul suburb. He was more familiar with the area because his brother had moved to the Twin Cities several years before we arrived as husband and wife. It seemed like the kind of place where one could live an ordinary life.

6

THE IMMEDIATE DAYS after meeting Madison for lunch, I continued to ponder her words, "Sherrie, I need you to finish your book." That day I swallowed hard because I understood this to mean she needed me. It also meant she needed me to be on a meaningful path. She needed me to move beyond my conditions and not get stuck in an unsatisfying life working for one of the top administrators. I understood she needed me to recognize I had power. My life could change if I really wanted it to.

After I talked to my minister-writer-friend, I knew my existence would begin to change. I spent my life keeping my same-gender attractions to myself. For the first time, I admitted this out loud and there was no taking it back. Admission is the first step to recovery.

• • •

JB and Jodi snapped themselves into their booster seats.

"Where are we going Mommy?"

"We're going to the park, but first I need to make a quick errand," I told them. I drove to my usual writing space, the chain bookstore. Madison's birthday was later that week, and I wanted to find the perfect card.

I found a small card with a few words. It said, "I hope your silent dreams come true." It was my perfect response to her perfect declaration . . . "I need you." It was my way of saying I knew what she wanted and I wanted her to have it. I wanted her to have me.

The three of us arrived at the park. JB and Jodi ran straight for the swings, and I sat on the bench with my card in hand. I wanted to explain the card. I wanted to be straightforward in my approach. What did a woman say to the woman she could very well see herself loving for a lifetime? I couldn't very well say those words, so I said nothing. I signed my name and sealed the envelope, and then went to push the kids on their swings. The twins were six years old. It had been less than three years since they became my children. The ache that entered my body shortly after their arrival had finally found healing, although I had not forgotten the cause of the ache. It had been only a few years earlier.

Three years earlier, I felt the November bite pulling myself out of the car, grunting a bit as I usually did when I exited a car because of my raggedy knee-joints. At the time, I was the fat girl selling out for skinny in a thin leather jacket and smaller clothes to fit my smaller body, at thirty-six pounds down that would rapidly diminish to fifty, sixty, to an ultimate seventy pounds less of me. You'd think the thirty-six pounds would have been something to celebrate for one finally losing weight after so many aborted attempts, after succumbing to the notion that weight loss would change my life. My life had changed for certain. I was bug-eyed with exhaustion and always so massively hungry, knowing that if I could withstand the physical ache of hunger each day, parts of me would continue to vanish. And that was the idea, really: to vanish. I was a new mother of children who needed me to be awake, when all I wanted to do was sleep. I begged the children to sleep at night, and did everything I knew how to promote sensations of calm and quiet in those squirmy, undeveloped muscles of theirs—the warm bath, the bedtime story about little farm animals on a cruise liner. "The moon is high, the sea is deep, they rock and rock and rock to sleep," I'd read. I sang songs about Jesus. Sang songs about love. And mothers loving their babies. And all the crap I was gonna buy them if they'd just hush and keep their tender little asses in bed. I yearned for sleep, but they would not let me, doing what two-year-olds did. Diamond rings and looking glasses held no appeal for my twins. I yearned for sleep, but my dearly beloved's absence kept me awake—coming in all hours of the night with new excuses each night for why I heard him climbing the stairs at two or three in the morning.

And I was a new mother. I could see their faces and compact bodies. They were there in front of me, within my reach. I knew they could see me too. They'd call out to me, "Mommy," but I was as mentally engaged as a single-cell organism. I was not with them in real time, though many times I would try to shake it off, drink cold water, and take many deep breaths to snap out of this perpetual state of lightheadedness. Even from that remote place, I could foretell my future regret about this present debacle: my failing as a mother. *What was all that longing about?* I questioned myself. I wanted this. I prayed for this. Greg and I bought the house on the dead end road, one block away from the cemetery, in order to have that large backyard where we would picnic outside like I'd seen all those white families on TV do all of my freaking childhood. I picked out the patio furniture and Greg purchased the grill.

This would be our first evening out without our children. The twins stayed home with my friend, who had come to babysit.

"I'm not used to seeing you like this," he said to me as we walked toward the entrance of our neighborhood TGI Fridays.

"Like what?"

"You know, so slender."

I walked several feet ahead of him because I was cold and needed to feel warm again. He walked as if he weighed five thousand pounds, hunched over, hands shoved into his pockets.

I was happier when I was fat. Happy with my fat. Fat and happy. Even naked. Even viewing the rolls of fat at my gut. Some people are bigger. Some people are smaller. I was one of the bigger. And when I wanted to feel overtly delicious, I thought I could. My mother once pulled tight bellbottoms up and over her big ass to stroll down Fulton Street, and the men fixed their eyes on her like she was the damn sunset. But who was I to Greg on this November evening? I wasn't the sunset, the moonlight, a flickering star twinkling in a darkened sky. Hell, I wasn't even a GE sixty-watt light bulb. In my natural way of being, I wasn't externally oriented. I never had the energy to be terribly concerned with the superficial. My riches existed within my internal life. And so my fat on most days went unnoticed by me, except when being exposed to my husband's wandering eye. His eye did not wander toward my likeness. His eyes wandered toward a smaller version of thickness. Like the version I happened to be that night at the TGI Fridays, only he stopped seeing me for so long I wondered if he had forgotten I was there.

So there we were, waiting for the cheese sticks, and I threw it out there right away, not wanting to waste another second.

"Where do you go at night?"

"Out."

"Out to bars?"

"Sometimes."

"To pick up women?"

"No!" He sat with his face twisted in knots.

He was being tight lipped and stingy with words, as he had been with his affection for so many months. He needed encouragement to talk and so that was what I had to do.

"You know," I said to him, "if our marriage should end, I think I should go for a more sensitive person the next time around. Just think about it for a moment. If you were set free from all of this, free from me, what would the next woman be like?"

"She would be tall," he said. I felt slightly relieved because I was five-foot-seven-and-one-quarter inches, which was taller than the average woman. But before I could respond, he clarified his meaning. "You're tall, but not that tall," he said. Well, how tall do you have to be to keep a husband these days? I was Meryl Streep in that movie she starred in with Jack Nicholson. Jack was sleeping with the ten-foot woman and Meryl was pregnant with her first baby. In the end Meryl hopped a plane to start her new life with her new baby away from the man who betrayed her. But how would my story end? Who could think of such things when they were in the process of icing over from the inside out?

"What else would she be?" Asking like a greedy masochist.

"Assertive... and spontaneous," he answered without hesitation.

I was no more assertive than my husband was emotionally expressive. I was a squirrel dodging shadows and footsteps. As for spontaneity, preparation was vital to one's own sanity. It wasn't sexy, but it was the truth. It used to be his truth. Since when did he grow a need for spontaneity?

"Are you seeing someone?" I asked again.

"No, Sherrie." He said with his eyes still on the table, not on his wife, his wife who used to mean something to him. This fucker was going to sit there and lie to me all night.

"Haven't I been good to you?" I continued like a Motown record. He agreed I had.

"Then I deserve the truth!" And the truth was what I got. He was seeing a ten-foot woman who was all assertive like some warrior bitch from another planet, flying to Vegas on whims for all kinds of spontaneous adventures. How was I going to compete with that?

He met her in June, the week of my thirty-second birthday. This was weeks before we had even learned about the twins.

"Why?" I asked.

"I don't know, Sherrie," was his response. No, "sorry." No, "I was an idiot. Please forgive me." I watched him bemoaning the loss of the girlfriend who dumped his pimply ass after finding out that he was married. There was no feeling for me that I could detect. No attempt at damage control. And I had to witness this. His torture. What about my torture? What about me?

"Why did you go through with the adoption?"

"Because I was ready to become a father," he said. I prayed for the spirit of peace to consume me because I was ready to take hold of my steak knife.

Suddenly, I found myself displaced without a home, in the Thomas Moore sense, the former Catholic monk I enjoy reading who said that home is "security, belonging, placement, family, protection, memory, and personal history." Now, I was homeless and a new mother of twins. And was in the midst of planning this kiddie birthday party. Why couldn't I have become a monk, instead of wife and mother? I could have written books with titles like *The Re-enchantment with Everyday Life* and written essays about the significance of gardens, but instead, I had to be another angry black woman coughing up the thorny stubs of rejection.

That was not me. I ordinarily didn't use words like motherfucker. Because I was, you know, the church type, and a pacifist, and a new mother who earnestly tried to entertain thoughts of higher virtues, who loved the proverb that says, "Those who plan for what is good find love and faithfulness." And that was what I had done for so many years, plan for good, and I wanted to be good. But yet, there I was sitting in a family-friendly restaurant and *motherfucker* was the only word that cycled through my consciousness.

I formed a smile and folded my hands to keep them warm, something he used to do. I forced my psyche to move in the direction of finding the good. Everyone had to co-exist with tragedy every now and again.

I demanded my legs, which had become blocks of ice, to pull my body up. I left the restaurant still hungry and feeling as if I had been abruptly dropped from the sky onto a glacier once known as home.

The years continued with Greg and I cohabitating on the same glacier, which never melted. I suspected it never would.

7

THE SUNDAY MORNING nine days after I met Madison for lunch, the day she said she needed me to finish my book, which, of course, I interpreted to mean that she wanted us to spend the rest of our lives together, was the last day of my week off from work. Greg agreed to give me one morning of writing before I had to return to work to clean out the inbox, make certain my supervisor had the right documents for the right meetings and showed up at the right place and right time. I needed to make my last few hours of vacation count for something. I found my usual spot in the bookstore. Unfortunately, it seemed as if all words in the English language turned to vapor. Many writing hours had been wasted away during those years of glacial living after finding out Greg was in love with someone else.

Three years later, at the time of meeting Madison, I no longer had tears for Greg.

When I arrived back home, the kids were in the middle of naptime. However, neither child was sleeping. Greg was on his way out as I walked up the stairs.

"See you later."

"See ya." I was past the point of expecting him to tell me where he was heading or when he would be back. I entered JB and Jodi's room. They both sat up quickly.

"Mommy!"

"Hey, guys." Both kids jumped out of bed and grabbed my legs. I kneeled down and pulled them close to me.

"Mommy, I want to tell you something." JB looked at me with a familiar look of fear.

"What is it, baby?" I ran my fingers through his hair and braced myself.

"Daddy is off the edge," he demonstrated by opening the palm of one hand and running his the tips of his fingers down the open hand from wrist to fingers.

"What happened?"

"He choked me."

"He what?"

"He choked me."

"Sweetie, this is very serious. You have to show me what happened. Did Daddy put his hand here?" I put one hand in the front of my neck. Five-year-old JB placed his fingers on the back of my neck.

"His hand was on the back of your neck? Your windpipe is in the front, so you would have been able to breathe."

"He squeezed it tight and I couldn't breathe."

"Were you scared?"

"Yes. It hurt and I couldn't breathe."

A year before, child protective services came to our house on Thurber Road when JB's preschool found blood blisters on his wrists. He had tried to cover his rear with his hands as Greg whipped him with his belt. When JB was asked by the adults at school about his blisters he told them, "Daddy spanked me 'cause

I peed on myself." Within days, two women from the county arrived at our house to investigate. Later, a letter arrived at our house stating the incident was found to be child abuse. We were given a warning. Greg agreed not to physically discipline the kids.

I wanted to believe the violent past was behind us, although it hadn't been gone long. It wasn't long before this when I wondered if my mind was diminishing from my lack of sleep, or did I have reason to be so mistrustful of the quiet shadows that sat in the corners of our home on Thurber Road? Lenora was the angel who was willing to shoo away the darkness that cowardly slid out of sight when she was present. In this time of need, she arrived at my house with three crucifixes. They varied in size and weight, and were made of different materials—one wood, two metal. I evaluated each of them as if I was deciding between blouses or pieces of jewelry, careful to make the right selection as if it were possible to make a wrong one. I had chosen the one that could fit in the palm of my hand. It was weighty and had sharp edges. I carried it with me in a pocket and frequently checked to make sure it hadn't fallen out.

Although I was barely a Christian by then, I believed the small metal offered some protection. Before bed, I held it firmly in one hand until I felt tranquil enough to succumb to sleep. Once I began to sway between dual levels of consciousness, I placed the crucifix on top of the Bible I seldom read. Except, of course, for those two Saturday nights a month when I waited until the last minute to prep my Sunday School lesson for the kindergarten class. Like the cross, my Bible was a symbol of a divine energy. I just held it close to me like it was the armor it claimed itself to be and, somehow, felt safer from harm. Although it was against my personal theology to ask God to provide me with the things I wanted, I felt it perfectly appropriate to ask for deliverance.

The mostly unread Bible I kept on my nightstand was a "Women's Bible," which meant it identified the female characters within the text and provided background to their historical and religious significance. Deborah led Israel to victory against the Canaanites when no man would lead. Priscilla was an artist and tradeswoman. Some believe Phoebe was a deacon in the early church and cite her as precedence against the silencing of women in the body of Christ. Then there were all those women who shared the name Mary. There was Mary, mother of God; Mary Magdalene, who was possessed by seven demons until Jesus cast them out of her; Mary the sister of Martha, who did not observe the traditional female role and sat at the feet of Jesus along with his disciples instead of helping her sister serve the men. That was the kind of righteous muscle I needed during my time of powerlessness. I needed a God who loved women, and who could obliterate evil at a mere thought.

I was the thirty-two-year-old tired mother of preschool twins and wife of Greg, and I was weak from hunger, but had little appetite. For some peculiar reason, we both rendered the decision over to Greg, who behaved like he was the unilateral decider who lingered between his wife in the northwest metropolitan area and the girlfriend in the southeast, saying one thing, doing another, and lying to us both. We were three nuts in one poisonous cluster and it was literally making us all sick, especially me, who easily became nauseous. Eventually, nausea turned into to abdominal pain that would make my eyes water. All of my life, I tended to carry my disappointments in my abdomen, and I had never been so bloated with disappointment.

Alone with my twins, we would sing songs of worship. "*The name of the Lord is a strong tower. The righteous run into it, and they are saved.*" My little ones were happy to sing with me. They were always happy to have their new mommy sit with them in their room at night and rub their bellies or backs as we sang songs in reverence to the Holy. I was in awe of the simple faith of my children, which made them quite eager to believe. After attending Vacation Bible School at my friend Holly's church, JB said he had a "Big, big, Jesus" in his heart, "who is walking around in there." He said it while making circular motions around the front of his torso. I pictured my son's Jesus sitting on a recliner, sipping coffee, and reading the newspaper.

"You do?!" I asked him.

"Yep!" he answered emphatically.

"I do, too!" added his twin sister, Jodi.

The twins would make their own request, asking, "Let's sing the one about diamonds."

"Good choice," I always said and began singing. *"Lord you are more precious than silver."* I was not a strong singer, but it was within my range and I could appreciate the anti-materialism subtext of the song. I held the notes as steady as I could. The kids would say I sounded nice, and I would blush at their compliment. I wondered if their foster mother ever sung with them at night. The children were certainly accustomed to bedtime prayers and often asked God to bless the whole world, attempting to name everyone in the whole wide world. I thought they probably would if they could.

After kissing the children, they would hold onto me, not wanting to let me go.

"Mommy's got to go to bed now. Mommy is so tired." In those moments, I spoke softly. Still, they held on even more tightly.

"We're never letting you go!"

My only escape was to tickle them under their arms until they lost strength. They would giggle and release me from their grip.

In my empty bedroom, I sat by the window, remembering my own mother, who battled the evil that lived in her house and whom she had nicknamed Delores. My mother was so spooked she could not name the wicked thing that haunted her. Not every woman betrayed by her husband goes crazy. Was that what happened to my mother, and was it also happening to me? Was I going crazy, or was it spiritual warfare the evangelical preachers were always talking about? Or was I simply malnourished and sleep deprived? Perhaps all I needed was a long nap and large bowl of creamy pasta with lots of grilled chicken that had been marinated in Cajun spices and olive oil. Maybe some spinach, and a nice tall glass of cherry Kool-Aid with real sugar, perhaps a few slices of toasted garlic bread with gobs of butter . . . I was probably just hungry after losing forty percent of my body mass. Anyone would be.

•••

On rare occasions I could catch Greg sitting with his conscience. An unexpected apology might be offered. "I'm sorry about all of this," was the most that he could say. If he could only understand what "all of this" really meant.

Some believers prayed for brokenness and viewed it as a necessary step before authentic repentance could be realized. Greg went to church more faithfully than I did and even criticized me when I refused to get out of bed on those "off-duty" Sundays when I didn't have to teach a class. He knew how this process was supposed to work. When a person was completely broken, he or she could be a new creature as the old things fell away. This made sense to me. I wanted to see the Greg I knew fall to the ground and shatter so finely he turned into sand. In his resurrection, a new person could be formed. This new person would be a better spouse than the asshole I'd married.

For me, he never groveled. In all of my years with Greg, I never witnessed his face wet with his own tears. The same man who found it difficult to smile also found it difficult to cry. He never laughed heartily. Often, he laughed with sarcasm, or cynicism, or some other source that was not humor. Was he capable of cracking, let alone, breaking, completely?

Sometimes he would compliment me and say I was a "good mother," "a good cook," "a good wife," or "a good person." But even in his compliments, I could feel his unanswered question on the back of my neck: Was I good enough? I could tell when my husband was sizing me up next to my competition, Sophia, the woman he described as tall, assertive, and spontaneous.

I knew Sophia was a drinker of MGM Gold because I would see it on the receipts I inadvertently discovered while searching through the pockets of his buttery leather jackets, smelling of smoke. I imagined him sitting at bars with his girlfriend who I figured to be the kind of woman who sat comfortably wherever she sat. I would never sit at a bar with Greg or anyone else, except when waiting for my take-out order at the neighborhood bar and grill. Then, I would sit uncomfortably on the high stool, hating the cigarette smoke, pretending to be interested in the Vikes. I never acquired the taste for alcohol. When I did make attempts to partake in a social drink, it gave me a headache and I'd need to lie down. I was a "softy." Sophia was not. She drank beer!

Other times, my husband shared more details. He missed his lover during those moments when he forced himself to spend time with me at the recommendation of our marriage counselor. I could feel it in my sickening gut. I might have been stupid because love can make you that way, but I wasn't dumb, for Christ's sake. I could sense Sophia's presence right there in our living room, sitting on *my* love seat next to *my* very thoughtless husband who was stupid in love, and dumb in general.

At times, I considered jumping off a bridge into some humongous nearby lake. However, I had a fear of falling and a fear of drowning. Along with my fear of fire, tornados, dogs, bunnies, roaches, all members of the rodent family, and being poisoned to death by my husband so he could collect the insurance money and escape overseas to live with his new spontaneous lover, Sophia. No, falling and drowning were not options. I was condemned to life.

I was very much alive and could not use drugs, alcohol, or even food, my usual substance of choice, to numb myself. Everything I felt, I felt intensely. Sometimes, it was intense devotion to my children. Sometimes it was rage. JB and Jodi got a taste of my late night fits. One particular night, Greg did not return home at the previously set time. I had gotten into the habit of watching his every move, digging through his pockets, sniffing out her scent with my very feeble sense of smell. I would question his intentions. "Where are you going? What time are you coming back? Will you be reachable by cell phone?" In our counselor's office, Greg promised me he would always answer his cell phone when I called. Bill explained that consistent behavior in such ways would help to restore my trust. Still, Greg always kept me guessing.

Jodi and JB both experienced their mother's outbursts, my backlash of frustration. I held onto blankets, pillows, coats, anything that I could ball up and squeeze. Other times, I escaped to the basement to pound the floor or myself: arms, shoulders, face, and head until I fell to the floor in exhaustion.

I had to find another way. Was there any truth to that saying about success and revenge? It is hard to say now, because I have gotten too old to believe in revenge. Revenge is just not a promising path. It's what people do when they have no idea how to process heartache. You can't do shit with heartache. All you can do is feel it until it eases. Then, you layer in some happy times until those grow and eventually become your new reality. In my forties, I believed in forgiveness. In my forties, I didn't believe in trying to get anyone to love me, which was even dumber than seeking revenge. When I was still in my thirties and still married to Greg, I tried to make him proud of me. I thought if he admired me, he could fall in love with me, not realizing that being in love was not the same as having admiration. I had admiration for Mother Theresa and Bishop Tutu. I had been in love with a girl name Anita—a long time ago. However, my thirty-two-year-old self was convinced Greg needed to see me succeed at something. The word "success" did not drop from the sky in a eureka moment, but it gradually made its way into my psyche until that became my focus. Success could make my husband fall in love with me for the very first time after fourteen years as a couple. If my plan did not cause Greg to fall in love with me, it would still be okay because I would have something better than a husband. I would have success. I knew some clichés were simply basic truths, like you catch more bees with honey than with vinegar, or a stitch in time saves nine . . . Actually, I had no idea what that the hell that was supposed to mean. A stitch in time saves nine what? Nine stitches? Nine fingers? Nine minutes? But living well, striving to achieve a personal goal was good logic. No one gets hurt when we do such things. Even if we fail, we win because hopefully, we'll learn something that could better prepare us for the next time we try.

I had an opportunity to read my work to a captive audience, so I was going to read an excerpt from what was then called *On Becoming Your Mother*. I purchased a new outfit a little more stylish than I was used to wearing. I chose to go monochromatic in a brown, snuggly-fit sweater and a faux-suede skirt trimmed at the bottom with a patchwork of various earth tones. I tried the outfit on with my new stretch boots. I was seventy pounds down and had new clothes and new make-up. I hoped outlining my lips and eyes could downplay the fact that my cheeks were a bit sunken in and my eyes were a little droopy from being sleepy and sad much of the time.

I read and reread the pages, hoping to let the words spring out of me with the intensity and sincerity with which they were meant. I would pause and breathe slowly before reading the words, "Soon, mother and babies are left behind." I wanted these words to penetrate Greg to his core and appeal to his sense of what was good. I wanted him to finally be sorry. I had the notion that the night of my reading could change everything.

One of my colleagues at work offered to keep the children for the entire weekend. The reading was on a Friday night. I took that day off work to start the weekend early. Greg did the same at my request, and I was surprised he obliged me. I imagined the two us going for dinner after the reading and taking our sweet time to return home because there was no thirteen-year-old baby sitter who needed to be home before it got too late.

I imagined Greg and I sleeping late on Saturday morning because there would be no hungry children at home waiting to be fed. The rest of the weekend could be spent in leisure. We would see movies that weren't Disney animations. At the advice of our marriage counselor, I promised myself I would not bring up the affair that was supposed to be over months ago, though all evidence said it was still going on.

Friday morning the kids were off, and my husband and I had the day to spend together before the reading that night. Greg spent most of the day at the computer. I rested most of the day. With time away from work and from kids, I was able to relax and enjoy the slow-moving day.

By late afternoon, Greg decided he had a taste for breakfast food. He suggested I run to International House of Pancakes to pick up food for both of us. I was bothered he wouldn't do the small chore of running the errand himself. It was getting late, and the later it got, the more nervous I grew about the evening. I hesitated for a moment, and he became annoyed by my hesitation. "It's the least you could do after I took a day off work for you." *What about taking the day off for us?* I wanted to ask him, but did not in a need to keep peace.

"All right, all right," I said before he could complain more. Caving in to his demands was a longtime habit. I called the order in before heading out the door in order to save time. He ordered his usual, country fried steak and eggs with a side order of pancakes. I ordered something for myself but wasn't too excited. I wasn't a fan this particular chain because I had an aversion to tasteless food, but it was what he wanted. The pleaser in me kept on pleasing. I had to get him to that reading, so he could shut up and be sorry for devaluing me over the past fourteen years.

The pancake place was busy and rather chaotic. The cash register wasn't working. Customers were agitated. I waited and waited for my order although it should have been ready by the time I arrived.

"Ma'am, would you mind waiting a little longer? We've been having trouble with our machines and your order got lost," I was told.

"Sure," I said empathizing with the poor young lady behind the counter who was trying to manage the commotion and the frustrated customers. I remembered my old days of broken-down machines, pissed-off customers, and endless lines when I was a young person in retail. It was obvious the staff were doing everything they could. There was no sense in joining the angry mob, surrounding the cashier and her manager.

I took a seat by the door and breathed a few deep breaths. I just allowed my mind to wander out of the door and out of the universe for a while. This was why traffic meters had never been a problem for me in those days. This time, however, I could feel the minutes slipping away, and it made me anxious. I considered walking out, but

I knew Greg was hungry and his mood worsened when he was hungry. I waited some more, not wanting to come home empty handed.

On a normal day, I was slow at getting ready, and Greg had always been even slower. He was always comfortable arriving late. I preferred arriving at least ten minutes early. On that evening, I wanted to be even earlier, at least thirty-minutes. I knew my stomach would be bouncing with jitters, which was why I had no interest in food. Anytime I had to stand up before people, my stomach would throw fits. I wanted to check out the space, claim a seat in the front, and perhaps read a passage before everyone arrived. I was prone to speaking softly. I wanted to practice lifting my voice so it carried throughout the room. I wanted to rehearse my pacing in order to make certain I did not speed through the words. What I really wanted was to perform the shit out of my piece and not allow one utterance to fall flat. There was no way I was going to do my best if I was frazzled, and my being late would certainly cause that.

"Okay," I said, getting up and speaking in my usual soft tones. I walked to the counter and stood next to the angry man who was shouting something about how "ridiculous" this was.

"Excuse me." The cashier did not appear to hear me. "Excuse me," I said a little louder.

"Oh, we have it right here, ma'am." She said handing me a plastic bag with Styrofoam trays poking out of it.

"How much?"

"Just take it, ma'am."

"Are you sure?"

"Yeah, just take it. We still can't get this thing to work." I followed the lady's orders and took my free food. I thought Greg would get a kick out of this. Free food.

Returning home, I put my own food in the refrigerator and placed the other tray on the kitchen table. Minutes into my shower, I heard Greg from the other side of the bathroom door.

"I didn't get my pancakes."

"What?"

"I didn't get my pancakes.

"Oh, I'm sorry. It was a madhouse in there. It was so crazy that they gave us the food for free."

"Yeah, and you're in such a rush to get to your *reading* you didn't give a damn about my pancakes." The way he said "reading" was like it was a totally senseless activity, a waste of anybody's good time.

I kept quiet, deciding I wasn't going to fight with him although I was feeling on edge. Fighting with Greg was bad business. I would always end up feeling worse than I did when I started. It involved too much shouting and too much crying. I could not cry that night because I would only end up with a headache and swollen, red eyes. This needed to be a good night, so I decided not to be drawn into the whirlwind of Greg's emotions. I stepped out of the shower and continued getting ready—lotion down, apply deodorant, slip into undergarments. I threw on a big T-shirt and walked into the kitchen to see if Greg was eating. I was going to provide a little bit of gentle encouragement to coax him into the shower. Greg was sulking at the table instead of eating. I assumed that he was still upset about the pancakes.

"Aren't you going to eat the rest of your food?"

"No. I don't want the rest of my food. I want my pancakes."

If I could not see the grown-ass man sitting before my very eyes, I would have assumed I was speaking to a whining toddler. I laughed under my breath and tried to contain myself.

"I know how we always have to move according to your clock," Greg continued. "Don't worry. I won't make you late, but I am sick of being rushed around by you." Greg wasn't going to be done until I reacted to his bullshit, and it was starting to work. The inner bonding agent holding me together was beginning to fail, and I was near stricken with cataplexy. *What a damn fool!* I thought. Then, I realized I was the bigger fool. Greg could not escape himself, but I had a choice.

"You know, what Greg? Don't come, because I don't want you there."

"Good," he said, as if he had gotten what he wanted all along.

"I don't want you at my reading," I reiterated. "And I don't want you in my life!"

I stomped out of the kitchen, doing battle with tears. It wasn't going to happen. He was never going to love me. By the time I made it to the other end of the house, I was lamenting fully. *I want out of this hell! I can't take it anymore!* I screamed internally, pacing, punching my thighs. I was flailing mad. I needed to throw something. I grabbed the plastic baby gate sitting outside of the twins' bedroom and flung it down the empty hallway. I went back to my room and shut the door. Moments later, Greg flung the door open, holding the baby gate.

"Are you trying to hit me with this?" He was enraged and shoving the plastic gate into my face.

"No!"

"Yes, you were!" He backed me into a corner. "I got something for your ass!"

He walked away and I continued to sob, not paying attention as to where he was going or what his intentions were. He returned to our bedroom holding the shovel we kept at the front door for shoveling snow off the front steps.

"I was not trying to hit you," I said. "I just threw it down the hall. You weren't even in the hallway. How could I have been trying to hit you? Please, put the shovel down!" Greg dropped the shovel and walked away. I sighed with relief. The worst was over. My life with Greg was over. I was going to figure out the leaving part later, but I had a more immediate task that evening. It was the only thing I didn't share with him. The one thing truly mine, unlike the house we lived in, the bank account we shared, and the last name we shared. I remember that day at the courthouse as we filled out the application for our marriage license. Did I really want to change my name? At first, I was opposed to it. I thought I would, at least, hyphenate my given name and include his. That was my original plan. At the last minute, I decided against it and became a Carter. Why, and how? I would spend many years attempting to answer that question and I've come up with only guesses.

• • •

Once, I heard that girls got their self-esteem from their fathers. My father was part-time because he had a new family. My parents divorced when I was four. Perhaps this played some role. Still, somewhere along the way I stopped wanting to identify either of my parents as the impetus behind my adult decisions. For some reason, it was easy to release them from my anger. From them, I felt acceptance, or belonging, or something. Although my mother was not expressive of her feelings, and my father was mostly not-present, I rarely questioned their love for me. Family dynamics could be so mysterious. Who knew why I felt the way I did? Maybe I just needed to. I don't know.

As a young girl, I was "touched" by an older brother. I was six and he was eleven. It happened over the course of a few months, or weeks. I was operating in child-time, so it is hard to be sure. He called it the rocking game. At first I thought it was innocent, and then it got creepy. I didn't like it, but I didn't want to hurt his feelings. One day, I gained the voice to stop it. He asked me if I wanted to play the rocking game, and I simply said, "No. I don't want to play that anymore," and left the room. After that, things were odd between my brother and me. I didn't trust him, especially after I began to develop. I wanted him to keep his distance. When he entered my room without knocking, I screamed with horror. "Get out of my room! Can't you knock! That's why you make me sick!" I never cursed in my mother's house, but I wanted to. He would act like I was a crazy girl suffering from PMS or something. "Chill out," he'd say as if I was overreacting. Later, when I was about fifteen or sixteen, I remember sitting on a dining chair in the living room, watching something on television. He came into the living room and stood next to me, wanting to see what I was watching. We exchanged some comments about the show. Then, he bent over and gave me wet kiss on the cheek.

"Stop! What are you doing?" I asked as I pushed him away.

"Nothing. Chill out," he said and left the room.

In those days, we would argue over nothing and everything. He was usually criticizing me about something. One night, I sat in the kitchen, eating a bowl of cereal. He suggested I should probably not be eating so late because it was probably the reason why I had begun to "put on a few pounds." I don't remember what I said in response, I only remember throwing my bowl of Cheerios at him. Of course, I was just being crazy again.

Watching the local news reports and studying police drawings of men accused of rape, I looked to see if they resembled my brother. This was how much I distrusted him. I saw him as capable of dragging unsuspecting women into dark alleys and taking all of his anger and hatred, or whatever he was feeling, out on them. I vowed to myself that, if I should ever see his likeness in one of those sketches, I would call the police. Then, I'd be sorry for not explaining to a responsible adult that my brother needed help a long time ago.

Two weeks before my brother died from leukemia, we argued. He wanted me to leave Greg. It seemed as if it was his dying wish. I told him it wasn't his business. Then I spilled everything I had been holding onto. What right did he have to tell me what to do with my life after what happened between us when were kids? For the first time, my brother apologized to me. He said he was the one who was sick, although he always acted as if I was the one who was crazy. My brother not only apologized for his inappropriate advances, but for all his criticism. He was fond of calling me names like clumsy ox (or the shortened version, clums-ox), four-eyes, turkey-neck, knucklehead, doofus, dumb-dumb, idiot. Did I integrate his words into my view of myself? Did I believe him? I suppose it would be conceivable to believe he was a thread in the making of my self-concept.

It was so confusing to the girl I was. I've gone through spurts of being desired by boys. In middle school, I was fully developed. I was nearly five-eight and one hundred and twenty pounds. Horny boys at school were after my body parts, not me. By high school, I was ignored by most boys. At the larger school, I was withdrawn and rather disheveled. I was more awkward than ever. Yet there was this weird attention from my brother who thought of himself as highly desired by "the ladies." He spent lots of time in the mirror, flexing his muscles. He drank protein shakes, lifted weights, and did push-ups every day. He was a football star in high school and college and was so incredibly cocky. "Your brother is a handsome guy," he would say to me, as if I was supposed to agree with him. I would just roll my eyes.

He always had lots of girlfriends. They were always pretty, middle-class girls from outside our neighborhood who were well spoken. What the hell did he want from his little sister? It just didn't make any sense. Some say girls are prone to marrying men who are like their childhood abusers. Is that what I had done? My current forty-something-year-old tears were telling me I might have been getting closer to the truth.

I went on my first date with a boy on my sixteenth birthday. Sixteen held some promise for me. I had my first job with my own money, and I had a boyfriend with a car. It was too exciting for words. Ishmael was gifted in math and science. He used a lot of big words I would later look-up later in a dictionary. He was also a lot shorter than me. Although we looked a little odd together because of our height difference, it didn't bother me. To me, he looked like the black Bruce Lee, with chiseled features and body.

However, this boy, who was two years older than I was, had a certain coldness about him. He always seemed distant, like he was trying to decide if he wanted to be with me or be somewhere else. It wasn't that way on our first date. On the first date, we both got in trouble for staying out too late. His mother waited for us in the front of our building. She said my mother called her because she was worried about me. I wasn't the type to stay out until midnight. I remember thinking my mother must have forgotten I was sixteen, which was just two years away from eighteen. Midnight seemed like a perfectly reasonable curfew to me. However, I thought I needed to give my mother time to adjust to my change. After all, I was the "baby" of the family, the youngest of eight. I went from being the girl who stayed close to home and by my mother's side to the girl who would have pizza with a boy and sit on the Brooklyn Promenade across from the Manhattan skyline and talk late into the night.

Ishmael told me he had heard about my suicide attempt the year before, and he became interested in me ever since because, apparently, it made me a *deeper* person than he mistook me for, or something like that. I told him I was done with all of that. I wanted to live and do something good with my life. We did agree on how much it sucked to be teenagers who always felt out of place. He was the brainy kid, and I was the shy one. That night Ishmael told me that whenever he heard the song "Blue Jeans," by Billie Idol, he thought of me.

Perhaps it was because I was no longer suicidal, but he lost interest rather quickly. According to Ishmael, I was overly accommodating and lacked drive, and it turned him off. He broke up with me. We got back together. We did this multiple times. He joined the Marines because he said he wanted to prove he was both physically and mentally strong. He knew he was smart, so he thought college possessed little challenge. He could always get to that later. When he wrote to me, I'd be happy to welcome the little Marine back, and then we'd break up again. The summer after I graduated from high school, he asked if we might get back together. I told him I was tired of the on-again, off-again. All of a sudden, he was interested and wouldn't let me go that easily. He continued to write. During my freshman year in college, he paid me a surprise visit at my college dorm room. He told me I was the best thing to ever happen to him. I looked at the twenty-year-old who was such a handsome little guy and knew for certain it was over. It felt great. Still, I would get an occasional phone call to see if I might have changed my mind. Before I married Greg, he showed up at my door, this time as a Gulf-war vet. He asked if I wanted to take a ride with him. I told him I was on my way to meet my fiancé. "I see," he said, taking a couple of steps back. "Well, see ya."

This thing with Greg was strange. At eighteen, I had been successful at getting Ishmael out of my system. At eighteen, before Greg sat his ass down at my table in the cafeteria, I wanted to explore my possibilities. I allowed myself to imagine what they were. There was still that thing I had with girls. I was still having those dreams of tender moments. I recognized I had an appreciation for my own sex. My dream-life reminded me of this. Many years later, I learned it was common for gay women to come out later in life. I wonder if it was because many young women were accustomed to denying our physical desires. However, physical desire was only part of it. There was also this huge emotional part that went unfulfilled. Perhaps it took emotional maturity to give ourselves permission to live a satisfying life. It was like those Revlon commercials when those aging beauties would swing their shiny hair and say, "I'm worth it." The way our lopsided world is set up to benefit one gender over the other, it can be hard for a young woman to embrace her worth.

Perhaps my early life was the perfect cocktail of events to put me in the predicament I was in at thirty-two. That night of the reading, I decided my putrid marriage was over. Somehow, I knew I had the capacity to be strong because I had been strong in the past. I had told other men in the past "no," because I'd had enough. I could do it again. This time, it took me fourteen years to do so, but I believed I could.

That night I chose to believe there was a loving God who was going to get me through all of it. First, I would get through the reading, and then, I would get on with my life. My heart rate started to slow. I felt something close to elation, like the other times in my life when I stood my ground . . . until my husband returned to our room. This time, he was holding a knife. I was frightened, but calm. I asked if he would put the knife down. He did not.

"Greg, please put the knife down."

"You want to die tonight?" he said in this crazy-man voice. "Well, you gonna die, bitch."

I asked the only God I knew at the time to please make that man go away. My breathing was heavy, but I told myself I would not trigger his rage. I knew I could not compete with his strength. Scott Peterson and his poor wife, Lacey, were in the news at that time, along with a string of other stories of men who had killed or were suspected of killing their wives. People did not think these men were capable of such horrific acts. People thought these were good marriages. These men did not become murderers until after they murdered their wives.

I jumped on the bed. Greg was blocking the doorway to our small bedroom. There was nowhere for me to go. I didn't want to cry. I wanted to reason with him, although I was terrified. I jumped up on the bed because I knew my legs were stronger than my arms. Early on I noticed his incredible upper body strength. He could lift things I couldn't even budge. My legs were going to be my best hope.

When I was young and dealing with the devil for the first time—what I mean to say is that I learned that Satan, the boogieman, and the headless monster living in my closet were no match for Jesus—I was told they would quake at the mere mention of his name. If, in fact, my husband was possessed by demons, then the God we once both worshipped could turn him into dust.

I pointed to my husband and started shouting. "Jesus is with me ... Jesus is with me. I rebuke you, Satan, in the name of Jesus ... Jesus," I repeated. "Jesus is not pleased with you, and he will destroy you!" I waited for a bolt of electricity to come down from the heavens and strike him down where he stood, but that didn't happen.

I jumped down off the bed and grabbed my phone. Where the hell was my crucifix when I needed it most? I hopped back onto the bed.

"Greg, put the knife down or I will call the cops."

"You'll be dead by the time they get here." I took my chances and dialed anyway. I spoke calmly to the female dispatcher, telling her my husband had a knife and was threatening to kill me.

"Where are you?" the dispatcher asked. Greg backed away and retreated to the kitchen. "Never mind," I said, hanging up the phone. I ran to the front of the house, where the front door was across from the kitchen. Greg was removing his country-fried steak and eggs with no pancakes out of the Styrofoam and onto a plate.

"Where's the knife?" I asked.

"Back into the holder," he said while placing his food into the microwave. "Don't worry, Sherrie. If I really wanted to kill you, you'd be dead already." I didn't have time to discuss it. I wanted to finish getting ready.

"Are you still going to that reading?" he asked me.

"Yeah," I answered abruptly and with an attitude of "of course, why wouldn't I?"

I still had to get ready. I pulled my braided extensions high on my head and began applying my make-up when I heard the doorbell.

That instant, I realized it was probably the police. I don't think I realized they would come anyway. Greg answered the door and stepped backwards as the police officers entered our home—one female and two male.

"We received a call from this residence," one of them said. Instantly, I felt guilty. *What have I done?* I asked myself as I saw Greg's body begin to cave into itself. He was no longer the man who just cornered me in our bedroom with a knife.

The female officer asked if there was another room where we could speak alone. We walked back into my bedroom and I spoke nervously. "He was just trying to scare me," I said.

"It's against the law to threaten someone with a deadly weapon," the officer said. "We have to take him. I want to give you a phone number. This organization helps women who aren't safe in their relationships." I actually questioned if I was a woman who wasn't safe in my relationship. I took the card from her hand and followed her out into the living room, where I saw the two male officers putting my husband into handcuffs. He was crying. All of these years, I wished he could cry for me and he never could, but I was still unsettled by his tears. I was afraid for him.

"Oh, my God. Oh, my God," was all that I could say.

"Sherrie!" he called. "Call my brother . . . please, Sherrie, call my brother." He continued to cry. He was broken, but not for me, not for the trauma he just caused me.

"I will," I answered through my own tears. I watched the police lower my husband's head into the back of the Charlie car, another black man being hauled away by the police.

I paced the floor. "It's going to be all right. Jesus is here. Jesus is here."

Seek the power-source when you're feeling completely without power. For someone who was barely a Christian, Jesus and I were good friends on that day. I continued to breathe. I washed my face, holding the cold rag over my reddened eyes. It hadn't been in my plan to cry that evening, but there I was. I didn't call the domestic abuse organization, and I didn't call Greg's brother. Is it customary for a victim of a crime to contact the family of the perpetrator so he can be bailed out of jail? At least at that moment, I didn't see that as my responsibility. I finished my make-up, did one more runthrough of the piece I was reading. It was the one about my mother, who had to raise eight children alone.

• • •

Mother

"I am grown. Get your own damn kids if you want to tell somebody what to do!" my mother always said when one of her children dared to act is if they knew better than she. Well, no one can claim I'm a disobedient child because I followed my mother's orders and got my own damn kids.

Three years ago was the last time I had heard my mother's voice.

"'ello, Alee," She attempted to call me by the name of one of her four sisters, Alice, the one sister who was still alive at the time, the one who was just one year older than my mother. However, my aunt hadn't talked for years since her stroke. My mother was not speaking very much, either. She had not been wearing her dentures, which caused her gums to shrink and mouth to cave in.

"I'm Sherrie. Your youngest daughter." When my mother looked up at me from her rolling lounge chair, I noticed the dark circles around her eyes had only gotten darker.

"What yur name, again?"

"Sherrie," I repeated.

"Dat a ni' name."

"You like it? You gave me my name, Mommy." Her face was soft. She opened her eyes wide when she looked at me. I felt as if she was pleased to see me, but wasn't sure why.

I was the daughter who left the house at eighteen for college and barely returned, barely called. Some have said a child never appreciates her mother until she becomes a mother herself. In my case, that was true. As a mother, I noticed her words coming out of my mouth, just as she had previously sprouted out of my widened hips and superfluous thighs. The mother I grew up with was not thin and frail like the woman she had become.

Her favorite sweater was an orange V-neck she wore with the gabardine that encased her feminine round, including the pouch that sat contently upon her lap when she sat. The brown and freckled skin within the V shimmered with white powder and a gold-plated medallion. Her earrings always dangled. Her Afro was always trimmed, and her bell-bottoms were always just a little too tight. Her strapless sandals clicked at her heels. Her extraordinary hips moved like a large body of water. With all of that swooshing and clicking down Fulton Street Mall, she was bound to sashay her way into some man's life. She had reason to hold her head up, but she rarely did. Her head was kept low. Her heavy eyes told truths beyond what she even knew herself. What good was the admiration of strangers when ultimately these men would be told of the eight children she had at home? "Wanting me means wanting them," she would have to explain to Mr. I-could-love-you-for-the-rest-of-your-life. The street games of New York City can do an aging ego good on lonely days, "but will the serious brothers please stand up!" I would have screamed for her if I understood then what I understand now.

And though I was too young to make much distinction between those who were serious from those who were plain fools, some gave the appearance of being serious, as in earnest, as in a fully grown adult male, serious enough for my mother to invite them home. The very few come to me now out of the dimness of memory.

Carlos was the Dominican brother who wore two-tone shoes. As a gift he once gave my mother a pair of matching two-tone pumps. I wondered if he might be the one despite the fact I found his choice of gift to be a little peculiar, and despite the fact that he barely spoke English. Though my mother is half Cuban, she barley spoke Spanish. Old Latina women would come to her in the street asking for directions or the time or who knows what, and she would respond in the only phrase she knew, "No Speaka Spanish." As I refocus my lens to see him more clearly, I think now that Carlos was not a boyfriend, but rather a shoe salesman. I recall an imprecise image of a box full of ugly shoes that sat in our apartment for several days, maybe more. They were all different sizes, and at least enough to fit eight sets of feet. Yes, I remember now. And I remember my brother Kyle and me deciding that no one could make us wear those hideous things. As poor as we were, we had the nerve to be particular, but we were often preoccupied with avoiding the appearance of poverty.

More than his shoes, what remains most clear in my mind is the way Carlos greedily took my mother in with his hazel eyes, and her obvious discomfort displayed by the frown she wore away from his gaze. He was trying to trade his sad footwear for love. For a moment, she must have considered it an adequate trade.

Robert came next, or perhaps first. The broad-shouldered man must have been a summer beau because I only remember him in sleeveless shirts that revealed his David Robinson-like shoulders and arms. He had a full mustache and the sideburns of Richard Roundtree. Maybe I'm just imagining these attributes. I suppose with so many years having passed, I couldn't identify Robert if he was standing right in front of me, but he seemed to be the kind of man who might be fingered by someone in a lineup. In my adult reconstruction of him, he appears looking something like Roger and Dee's daddy from that '70s TV show, What's Happening! *In any case, Robert went away just as Carlos did before him, or maybe it was after him, and I dared to ask my mother why because I disliked the thought of her being without a companion. I should have known her answer would simply be that she'd rather not talk about it.*

Not talking was my mother's way, which was why I thought Sam would finally be the one who would stay. I cannot say that he ever spoke one word to me, but I was fond of him. He certainly had an easy manner, and appeared to embody a measure of decency, which I couldn't say for Carlos and Robert. Sam worked for the City of New York. What he did for the city, I can't recall, and I'm not sure if I ever knew. I knew he had the same job for more than twenty years and had plans to work another ten years before he retired. I imagine he would have retired years ago now, to someplace warm, quiet and slow. I thought my mother would be the perfect mate for a man like Sam. She would return home from Atlantic City with bags of salt water taffies she would share with me. She would carry home the stuffed animals he had won for her at the Coney Island game booths. But what I appreciated most about Sam was that he did not call her Dot like everyone else, but Dorothy.

A time or two, Dorothy would make a meal and after her youngest children would eat and scatter about, the two middle-aged adults would sit without chatter, as if they were prepubescent teens who hadn't a clue about date-talk. I know this, because I made a point of hovering within earshot. I remember him saying once the meatloaf was juicy, and my mother said it was the tomato sauce. Sam nodded and the rest of the meal was eaten in near silence. He mumbled a thank you and my mother began to collect the dishes in the gentle and meticulous way she did things when peace was present. Sam lasted for a few seasons, perhaps even the same season twice, much longer than the others. When he went away, I had the nerve to ask why. This time she gave me an answer: "I'm not the type of woman to keep company with a man who will not marry." My mother was the type of woman to use phrases like "keep company." She was a former Burgeon Street beauty, the youngest of the five Fernandez girls who were penniless, but well groomed, pressed and tidy with multi-ethnic island-heritage hair. And though my mother was one of the darkest sisters with the kinkiest head of hair, there was still something almost exotic about her in the eyes of a few useless men. She was considered nearly as pretty as her sisters Helen and Alice, who more or less looked Puerto Rican. Under the bizarre hierarchy of color, less being more, the Fernandez sisters reaped fractional benefit from the times in which they were living, the post-northern migration/pre-afro-pick era when too many of us (us meaning anyone who's ever lived in a racialized society) were too messed up to see beauty clearly in all hues of the Diaspora. All five of these women, Dorothy and her sisters, found southern gentlemen who promised to love and care for "their girls" for as longs as they all remained girls . . . which of course was not the original promise said before God, the Universe, and at least two witnesses, but a promise is only as good as the mouth that speaks it. And by the time enough years would pass for the sisters to have their Brooklyn apartments filled to their paint-chipped ceilings with children, four out of five of them would have to learn to be gifted in "the art of losing," in the Elizabeth Bishop sense. Only Eleanor, the one considered the most desirable of all five, stayed married 'til death. It was her death from a ruptured aneurism when she was thirty-three.

When peace was present, Dorothy was as tender as her belly. Then again, sometime after 11:00 p.m. she might become Hurricane Dot, as we named her, rising from her slumber while the children waited quietly without making any sudden moves. Soon we would hear the clang of mettle smashing into metal as pots slammed into the kitchen sink. She'd be mumbling to herself about how she "don't have nothin'," her red and swollen eyes nearly shut from sleep, but always displaying her rage. We all did our best to stay out of her vision in fear of getting impaled. "Tear up every damn thing . . . Can't keep shit . . . Eat me out of house and home," she would mutter while sweeping the hell out of the floor, shoving chairs out of her way. Many nights she woke to find we were the same ungrateful children she knew we were before she'd fallen asleep while watching reruns of The Odd Couple.

In the late night hours, we would become gluttonous house rodents devouring all morsels not intended for our consumption. In the midst of one of her midnight fits, one of her eight children might dare to tell her to just calm down, as in, "I'm gonna do the dishes, Ma. Just calm down." Dot would holler back, "Don't you tell me to calm down. I'm grown. Get your own damn kids if you want to tell somebody what to do!" I would attempt to calm her down with cheap affection, like the time I kissed her on the cheek with lips sticky from the no-name syrup. I only succeeded at turning a category-two storm into a three or four as she threatened to blow us right out of downtown Brooklyn to the place where nasty little children go.

Screaming mothers in my neighborhood were as common as bodegas and check-cashing places. I woke to the high-pitched shrieks of the woman upstairs scolding her children for doing unthinkable things, just unthinkable, like neglecting to refill the ice trays in the freezer. I've seen mothers in grocery stores drop their kid's pants and wallop their exposed behinds as they pleaded upon unsympathetic ears. Alice Walker said that her mother's Gregration was "ragged head Gregrals with fist as well as hands." Their hands made strong, she said, by working in the field and dragging heavy mops across someone else's kitchen. What of my mother's Gregration? Who were these women fussin' and cussin' urban women?

My mother and her neighbors had as many babies as God and nature would allow. And sooner or later, mother and babies were left behind. It was 1974 when my father said that, if he stayed, he would only end up drinking himself to death. I remember the men who did succeed at drinking themselves to death. I'd watched them stumble around the neighborhood with their bellies jutting outside of their T-shirts, falling asleep on benches, pissing behind trees, and banging on doors because their wives done changed the locks.

Soon, we'd find the obituary hanging up in the lobby of our building. Mr. X, Y, or Z former Navy Man, Korean War Vet, former transit worker, or postal clerk, or dock worker, preceded in death by his mother, father, and two brothers who also died too young. Mr. X leaves behind an impoverished wife and umpteen children who ask for donations to cover the cost of his burial. This is what my father's death may have been, cirrhosis of the liver, after years of passing out in the street and vomiting in trashcans chained to benches. He chose to leave instead.

I, as a baby of such a mother, am reminded of quiet, decent Sam, the one whom I thought would stay, and wonder if he thought I was a girl in need of a daddy because I still had growing years ahead of me, and because I was always sniffing around them like some hungry house pet. If I could, I would tell you, Sam, all I wanted was to take in Dorothy's fragrance as she clicked her way out the front door on a Friday night swaying like the Atlantic Ocean after smelling the flowers you just gave her. On those nights, I would stay up late waiting for her and watch you hold her balance as she stepped out of your car. I watched from the window as you kissed her goodnight. It was especially satisfying because it was right in front of my mother's former adversaries, the women of Farragut Projects who once worked overtime to pique my father's curiosity after their own husbands left or died.

I would irritate her with questions. She would tell me you were a good person, though I could see that for myself. Once, I rubbed her back with ointment as she ached from sitting too long on the beach with you. She was too busy being at peace to notice her own skin burning. When peace was present, Dorothy moved slowly. She might even hum at bit before and after 11:00 p.m. She shared her salt-water taffies and her stories with me, however little she was willing to tell. She held her head up just a bit more and her eyes appeared less weighted. I watched her slip into the soft leather slippers you just gave her for Christmas and knew it had been way too long since she had known such comfort.

8

NINE DAYS AFTER MEETING Madison for lunch, my son told me he was scared of Greg. It was my last morning of writing before having to return to work. I entered the home on Thurber Road where I still lived with Greg, JB, and Jodi. Some would see our collection of four—man, woman, boy child, girl child—and assume we were a family. Only the inhabitants knew better. I did not wait to calm down before calling Greg on his cell phone.

"What is it?" Greg asked.

"JB said you choked him."

"I did not choke that boy. Why do you believe everything they say?"

"He's afraid of you."

"That boy is afraid of his own shadow."

"I told you JB is a sensitive boy. You can't parent a sensitive boy too hard or they can become hard themselves." Ever since my high school psychology class I knew the difference between an authoritarian parent and an authoritative parent. Authoritarian parents were enforcers of the law. Authoritative parents provided structure and boundaries, but were not afraid to provide some choice and wiggle room for their kids to grow. When sensitive children were raised by authoritarian fathers, they tended to follow what they'd been taught. I wanted to tell Greg that was what probably happened to him. His stern father squeezed the tenderness right out of his body. "Remember the article I showed you," I continued. "Child protective services were already at our house."

"You think you know everything. You don't!"

"I know you are an asshole, and that's all I need to know!"

"There's something else you might want to know. I bought a gun, and when I get home I'm going to shoot your ass!"

"I'm leaving, Greg!"

"So leave, bitch. Nobody wants your ugly ass anyway, but I will kill you before I let you take my kids!" I still hadn't gotten used to Greg's threats. *I'm gonna put your head through that wall! I'm gonna break you in two! I'm gonna stab you. I'm gonna shoot you.* He knew just what to say to push me away, which I later realized was his ultimate objective. Did he have a gun? Would he shoot me? I was beginning to believe Greg really did want me dead and if he could find a way to end my life without punishment, he would. Often, he expressed his disgust toward me while declaring his love for the kids. "Just because I can't stand you, doesn't mean I don't love my kids." It all came to a head in that moment—the cheating, the violence, and the simple lack of care between us. Why was I still there? What was stopping me from leaving?

I gathered JB and Jodi. I thought it was best we not be home when Greg returned. I wanted to give him time to cool off. That was his typical pattern, to blow up like a madman and then retreat inside himself. I needed to put distance and a little time between us in order to find my own inner calm. I didn't have a plan. I just knew it was time to start the process of leaving. The kids climbed into their booster seats in the back of my station wagon. We were invited to a picnic day sponsored by the black alumni association, to which the African-American staff and faculty were also invited. I hoped Madison would be there.

I could smell cooked meat as I approached the quad and from a distance, I could see the inflated house for children to wear themselves out.

"A jumpy house! A jumpy house!" Jodi screamed. "Can we, Mommy?!"

"Just remember to kick off your sandals before you climb in," I instructed. The kids ran full speed for the blow-up play house.

The adults gathered underneath a garden tent. It must have come in handy in the light rain that passed through just before I arrived. Madison was there in her usual summer attire, khakis and a T-shirt. From a distance she looked as if she was entertaining the small group of people gathered around her. She was in the middle of her shtick. Later, I learned she battled between becoming a sociologist or a comedian. She chose academia for its stability. I watched the older and distinguished African-American alums laugh heartily at Madison's antics. The young professor must have been a source of pride and a symbol of how far we'd come as a people. However, instead of behaving like a somber scholar, she was more like the female version of the comic Sinbad, a preacher's kid known for clean humor about his strict parents.

Later, Madison told me her introversion was to blame for her humor. She told jokes when she was nervous. When she noticed me, she excused herself from her approving audience.

"I wondered if you were going to be here today," she said.

"I wondered if you were going to be here, too." We both reached out for a quick hug.

"Thank you for the birthday card," she said with her gigantic smile. Madison was good-natured. She smiled broadly and laughed like a person full of contentment. Was I too dull for her? Would I dampen her inner joy?

"You're welcome. Did you have a nice birthday?" I tried to match her lightness of spirit.

"I did, although it was hard to see my mom and auntie leave."

She was alone in a state without any family. It was only her second year in the Twin Cities. My thirteenth year in the Cities was the luckiest one yet—it was the year I fell in love with Madison.

I sat with Madison and the dean of students. Madison jumped up when her number was called as the winner of the raffle drawing for a modest prize.

"Yeah!!!" She yelled as if the Packers, her favorite team, just won the Super Bowl. Then she ran to get her prize like a contestant on *The Price Is Right* who came on down to play for—*A New Car!* She hugged the presenter of the gift, the executive director for Institutional Diversity, like he was Bob Barker. Everyone laughed.

"She is so funny, isn't she?" said the dean of students, who sat at our table.

"She's crazy," I said, shaking my head. After showing her appreciation for her prize, she said she would like to donate it back in hopes a student would win it.

At the end of the event, Madison walked with Jodi, JB, and me across campus toward the blue station wagon.

"How have you been?" Madison asked.

"I'm fine. I decided to leave my husband."

"Really?" She did not sound surprised.

"Yes. I'm done."

"If you ever need to talk, feel free to call me." She wanted to write down her phone number. I told her there was no need. I worked for the numero uno vice-president and had access to all faculty contact information. I promised to call.

• • •

The night of the picnic, Greg and I had little to say to one another. I had grown even more skittish of him. I appreciated the alarm system we had installed in our home just weeks after we moved in. It was less about the potential robbers outside and more about the angry man inside from whom I desired protection.

I stood by the front door as I talked to Greg. The system was on so all I had to do was open the door and walk out without turning the alarm off and the police would be there in minutes. I did not have a speech prepared. However, I did not want to set Greg off.

"Greg, I think we should separate."

"You and I are different. You give up too easily," was his response. I made the calculations in my head. Eighteen years of no love. Eighteen years of cruelty. Eighteen years of being told I was ugly and stupid. Eighteen years of his rage over the littlest shit imaginable—not closing cabinet doors, forgetting to turn off the computer. Eighteen years of him fucking other women or wanting to fuck other women. Eighteen years of being told nobody else would want me. Eighteen years of believing he was right about me. How many more years would I need to give?

"Well, maybe if we took some time apart, we can work on ourselves and try again later," I said. I did not want to argue with Greg. I was done arguing with Greg. I needed to leave, but I had to ease him into the idea. I wanted him to believe there was a chance we could reconcile, in order to leave without confrontation.

I even offered to talk to his most recent lady-love. "Perhaps you can make things work with her."

Greg confessed that he gave up the chance for sweet love with Sophia for stability with me. I reminded him I would've let him go.

"I guess I wanted to have my cake and eat it too. Now, I've lost both of you," he said.

In the next four weeks of our lives together, life at Thurber Road was relatively calm. At times, Greg seemed relieved we were parting ways. Other times, I could sense fear in him, which made me anxious. I had to reassure him I would consider trying again, although there was no way in hell I meant it.

JB and Jodi were about to begin at their new school in what was soon to be our new community. Relieved that we made it to that point, the first day of school signified we were one step closer to making the transition to our new life.

Greg said he wanted to have some say about which school they would attend, so he went with me to the Saint Paul school placement office. The schools with the best reputations were full since spring. In late summer, we had to pick from what was left so we selected the school located across the street from what was going to be our new apartment.

Sitting in the placement office with Greg, apprehension thinned my breathing. I expected Greg to make it difficult, yet I moved through the multiple steps of our separation without much resistance from him. The first step was finding housing. The second was finding a school for the kids. The third step was scheduling the movers. Fourth: pack. Fifth: move.

9

MADISON AND I were the same side of two individual coins with similar needs. We were both dreamers. We were both deeply in touch with our emotions. We both wanted to be heard. We both wanted to be free from an oppressive past. We both allowed ourselves to cry, although I cried more. We both wanted to be touched with tenderness. We both wanted independence. We both wanted to enjoy the satisfaction that came from being fully who we were. In some ways, we both wanted protection. We were both the protected and the protector. It was equality like none other I had ever experienced.

From a distance, I saw a woman taller than I, with hair that was shorter than mine. Up close, she spoke without words, saying, "I will take a risk and love you." Before then, I had only known that look in dream-life, but never in real life. Her face was generous and daring. It said she knew I had the ability to hurt her, but she was going to trust I wouldn't. I wondered what she read in my face when she first saw me up close, close enough to hold, close enough to kiss. I wondered if she could see how much I wanted to find acceptance in her kiss and how amazed I was when she gave this to me. I arrived a bit shaken with hurt in my body, strapped to my back, churning in my stomach, weighing me down, exhausting my spirit. I arrived reliving a nightmare, begging God to make it stop. I arrived like my own head of damaged hair in need of replenishment, like my dying winter skin. I arrived wanting reassurance that she was there, that we were in this life together. What I had done for love, I would never have to do again. All I had carried might fall at my feet as I stepped away with her towards love, acceptance, and extraordinary peace. She welcomed me and I took the risk to love her.

It took eighteen years to make the decision to leave Greg. Eight weeks after the decision was made, JB, Jodi, and I left the house on Thurber Road and moved into a small apartment in Saint Paul across the street from their new elementary school. We were about twelve blocks from Madison.

For eighteen years, I believed erasing Greg from my life meant erasing discord. After meeting Madison, I developed mental images of a new progressive family, girl child, boy child, and two moms—a rainbow family full of goodness and light. My capacity to fantasize surfaced early in childhood. I could produce slides upon slides of an idyllic life. I've created so many scenarios, all in my head. As much as I had suffered from attempting to realize my fantasies, I was sure I wouldn't have survived my early life without my fantasies. It gave me something to work toward.

While still married to Greg, I continued to work for fulfilling the vision of my youth, to live an admirable life, raise admirable children who would further the race. I remember how I hastened through the process with focus while time lingered at its own pace, as it usually did when all bodies were frozen and our workday precludes us from the experience of fleeting daylight. Something in my shoulders melted along with icy lakes. Something at the core of me grew in unison with Midwestern perennials. I could not imagine a Minnesotan who did not have a deep and abiding affection for the month of June. The beginning of summer just happened to be the month of my birth. I did not feel lucky in most things, but since I was a child, I always felt I had a very lucky birthday. It was June, and everything was possible, including my long-awaited plans. I pulled back the blinds that covered the large picture window in our living room and saw those ridiculous daylilies blooming in the shadow of the giant evergreen that stood in our yard on the corner of Thurber and Xerxes in Brooklyn Center. The space that I occupied, the 1964 rambler, was well aware of my plan. Yellow and crimson fish swam in the blue sea in the hall bathroom. Mickey and Minnie Mouse adorned the walls of what was going to be a child's room. It was the work of the previous owners. The laminate counters in the kitchen were wiped clean and free of clutter. The structure beamed proudly, ready to fulfill, again, its purpose for being built: to house a family. Before the Carters, a family of seven had resided in that house. A woman who shared my name with a different spelling lived there with her husband for seventeen years. Eventually, they filled the space with their black lab and four small children. The other Shari was deeply attached to the house. Of course, she was excited they were moving into the big log house they always dreamt about having in a smaller town outside the Cities. Still, on the day of closing, tears welled up in her eyes at the thought of leaving behind the place where so many cherished memories took place for her and her husband. They had lifelong friends in the neighborhood and in the beginning, Shari used to stop by when she was in the area to visit the house she still loved. I happily welcomed her in. She approved of my choice of warm browns and burgundy. She complimented my window treatments. She asked me if we were enjoying the house and if we would be doing anything with the very large sandbox in the back yard. She reminded me that the neighbor's cats used to pee in the sandbox, so we probably wouldn't want to let our children use it after they arrived. There wasn't a person who didn't know of our plans to adopt children. Before Shari's family lived in the house, the original owners occupied it for nineteen years. The husband was a builder and had a hand in building our house and other houses in the neighborhood. What could give a homeowner more pride than living in the house that he or she built? I hoped that history of the house would teach us what we needed to know about stability and commitment. Perhaps the house had special powers and all who lived there would be aided by its magic.

At the time, I did not realize how much time I was spending in my head. My favorite pastime was logging onto the website for Hennepin County's Waiting Children. In the year of 2002, children of color made up five percent of all Minnesotan children, but fifty-six percent of children who were under state guardianship were children of color. I lived my whole life knowing there were so many problems facing poor communities of color, but this was one problem I determined to address with my hands, my heart, my resources, and my home. We were working through the African-American Adoption and Permanency Planning Agency, a nonprofit adoption agency whose mission was to find parents willing to adopt these children. Driving to work, I heard the advertisements on Solid Gold Soul radio station. In my new Ford Taurus station wagon, I listened to the brother who played R&B oldies, encouraging his audience to consider foster care and adoption in between funk jams and ballads from Earth, Wind and Fire and Curtis Mayfield. In one moment, I could be singing along to the sounds of my childhood—then look up to see a billboard of a striking black child with a pleading face. I absorbed it all, every advertisement, every interview aired of the single black grandmother who provided a home for motherless children. We moved into that house with the raspberry bushes during the first days of Y2K. Since the planet was still in orbit, I immersed myself in the adoption process. I thought the house on Thurber was built with the intent of housing children. We purchased the house with the same plan in mind. The time had come.

We had space in our quiet rambler, which seemed almost too quiet at times. Our home seemed to crave the sound of children.

After a day of work, I used to log onto the website for Hennepin County's Waiting Children, viewing the photos and reading the tragic stories beneath. I wondered which one might find someone like me suitable, a quiet and anxious woman most at peace when she could spend all the live-long day on a feather bed of imagination. This was both my best and worst attribute. One young girl looked back at me with her index finger resting on her upper lip as if she was evaluating me. "I don't know about this one," I imagined her saying back to me. "This one seems a little odd."

When I went to work at that little nonprofit to peddle business camp to high school juniors and seniors, my co-worker, Irene, a woman raised in Chicago as the daughter of Polish immigrants, was like a walking percussionist, her words beating my eardrums like mallets. She had photos pinned to her cubical wall of two very beautiful children of color. My first thought was that they were bi-racial, and if Irene was their mother, their father must have been black.

"Are these your children?" I asked.

"Yes. Adopted. Foreign-born. My son is from South America and my daughter is from Southwest Asia," she responded in an automated tone which made me think she had answered in the same manner many times.

Eventually, I shared with Irene my own interest in adopting children. Without hesitation she blurted, "All people who adopt children are emotionally messed up. Believe me, I know from experience." It took a moment before the smashing cymbals stopped vibrating in my ears. Everything Irene knew, she knew from experience. It was like the day she warned me to watch my back after my father-in-law died, for "when men lose their fathers they also lose their fucking minds. Believe me, I know from experience. They become consumed by thoughts of their own death."

The fear of death must have corroded Greg's skull and altered the chemistry of his brain. His father was dead and his wife wanted badly to turn him into a dad. He would no longer be the child.

Just as I examined each child on the waiting child website, and wondered about who those children really were aside from the six sentences devoted to each of them, I felt them wondering about me. "What's your story? Why should I allow you to be my mother?" Waiting children are often deemed as challenged, at best, and at worst, irrevocably damaged. But was Irene right about waiting parents? What were our issues?

I was waiting to be a mother and thought I should do some living in the midst of the waiting. On Thursday nights, I joined Holly, Brandon, and Lisa for Salsa lessons at Four Seasons Dance Studio. Our teacher, Rebecca, smoothed her frizzy hair into one ballerina bun on the back of her head. She was a small classically trained woman with a loud voice that bounced off of the walls of her studio as she counted in Spanish. We paired off in male/female duos, and I found my favorite partner in a thin man from Loring Park who told me I was light on my feet. Imagine that, as large as I was. But he was a good student who stepped when Rebecca said step, unlike that other little guy who flung me around the floor in opposition to the beat as if he was trying to prove he could handle a plus-sized woman. If I tried to get the twirp to dance to the beat, then I would be in violation of the first rule in couples dance, the man always leads. It didn't matter if he was five feet tall, rhythm-less, and danced with vengeance written all over his small-boned face.

On Saturday morning, I met with my writing friends, Lenora and Libby, to share our work. Lenora and Libby grew up in places I would have once considered to be in the middle of nowhere, but their stories made it somewhere for me. I saw Libby driving her father's tractor, blowing cottonwood from her face. I heard the howling coyotes as Lenora slept in the woods. The Brooklyn in me sat in wonderment of their lives.

During adoption summer, I continued my job of advising students. I read. I wrote. I danced. I exercised and saw less of me each week. I dined with friends. I dined alone. I went to church. I prayed and read my Bible. But no matter what I was doing with my body and some parts of my mind, no matter what impression my spirit seemed to be resting on or wrestling with, I always found space in my inner world for children. I tried to communicate with my future child and prayed he would somehow hear me.

Dear Child of Mine,

There is a message I pray will be delivered to you today, naturally or supernaturally. I don't know if it came to me in a dream or how it came to me. But I discovered that time passes and time frees. I think messages are whispered in the atmosphere in cloudy puffs and somehow I was lucky enough to have some of the good ones land in my ear and travel secretly through my system. I'm whispering to you right now. Just like it came to me in a whisper that I should find you. My desire to find you commenced way down in my soul, and soon reached its way into my consciousness, and suddenly a cosmic portion of my life made sense, my purpose, I mean, something I was being called to do. It all came in nearly inaudible utterances that an untrained ear may never hear. But it was extraordinarily comprehensible to me, and I remembered what it said in Jeremiah, "Before you were born, I set you apart." I think that God set me apart just for you and you were set apart for me. And though I may not be your mother naturally, I am certain I am your mother supernaturally. And for me, that is a more alluring choice.

When I was small, sometimes the whisper would tell me just to wait. I was good at waiting, very patient, even in hospital waiting rooms, even in long lines at the grocery store, even at the welfare office. I sat very still next to my mother and listened to my mother recite the same answers to the same questions. How many people in your household? How many under the age of eighteen? Whatever papers she needed to materialize, she would. My mother was good at putting ducks into rows, something I never acquired. My ducks are in messy piles under beds, on top of refrigerators, shoved into overstuffed cabinets. My ducks are not always retrievable at the moment I want to retrieve them. My skill was in waiting. If I wait long enough, the right duck would show itself sooner or later. I'm not nearly as good at waiting as I used to be. I think it is because I now know that, all of this time, I have been waiting for you.

So, child, I want to send you the message of being good at waiting. Do not act hastily unless the alarm has sounded and the building is on fire. Do not be too loud, otherwise you'll miss it when the whisper comes. Be still long enough to allow it to enter your system. Be still long enough for you to know what it is telling you. You will know it when it blows through a cracked-open door, even a rickety one. And when it penetrates you, you will know that it is stronger than hope.

I liked it when I heard that reverend say there's a difference between hoping and having hope. When you have hope, the hope belongs to you. The ownership makes it real, almost tangible, just like you are real and almost tangible. I talk to you all of the time in my mind and in my dreams. I don't know if you are a boy or a girl, of three or ten years. But the nearness of you weakens me and brings me to moments of acute grief, and the nearness of you fills me with delight, like a giddy junior-higher squirreling over Teen-Beat *magazine.*

My waiting has been compromised by what I've been able to accomplish. What have I accomplished? As I have said before, nothing spectacular, but simply amazing: adulthood. I pray you will some day find things to be amazed about after we become your "forever family." That is what they'll call us when they write about you in the success story pamphlets. I like that term. It means that, when you come, you will bring forever with you.

Last night before sleep, I watched myself holding you, because you had fallen asleep on the couch. In a half-slumber, I lifted a little boy, feeling your lightness of weight, your slender build in my arms as I carried you to your room and put you in bed. I kissed your face to see if you might wake, but you did not. I left you only to know that tomorrow we'll meet again. Another night, in my sleep, I dreamt you were a woman. I walked into a room, with sheer curtains being carried up by a soft wind. Walking past the curtains, I stepped onto the terracotta patio and peered across the tropics. You startled me when you cried out, "Mom!" I turned and saw the most beautiful shade of brown, with thick and healthy hair, and the sweetest round face, brilliant and piercing eyes. You were shorter than I was and had incredible buoyancy and optimism about you, and you were happy to see me. No, you were ecstatic to see me. Can you imagine? We hugged and laughed and cried as if we had not seen each other for some time, not years, not months, but more time than what's tolerable.

Time passes and time frees. I pray that you hear my whisper. You will enter the world of a praying mother. I believe there is a Creator who speaks and listens. Religion is scary and complicated. It unities and it divides. It saves and it massacres. It comforts and it ruins. At times, I have been uncomfortable with carrying the label Christian. In the evangelical world I may be seen as being a lukewarm believer fit to be "chomped up and vomited out." Once, I think I thought I'd rather be lukewarm than so hot that I burn bridges, burn myself, burn ideas not my own, burn truths not my own. But even in my rebellion, I realize now I have never been lukewarm because I prayed with full certainty I am heard and I am cherished. I prayed with full certainty you are heard and you are cherished. When I pray, I send up words, and the Divine sends back hope and presents the priceless elements on a crystal platter. There are still many things left uncertain. I don't catch all the cloudy puffs, only a select few. A select few is all most of us get, and we must treat them with great care and protect them with our very lives. Waiting is a good one for both of us now, though I very well know it is easy to be impatient when you're waiting for forever.

I love you deep down in my soul. This love for you was placed there at my birth. Stay warm this season. I'll see you soon. ~Mom

• • •

The summer before adoption summer was similar to most other summers. I think I always had the hope that getting away from our ordinary lives would propel Greg and me to a higher level of love. We would just load up the car and drive out of the city. I'd make sandwiches for the drive, pack Chips Ahoy, Doritos, and bottled water. We'd collect our favorite music, jazz and gospel. Kirk Franklin was always in tow. We dreaded being left with whatever FM radio played outside the city limits. I would buy new lingerie just for our trip. We'd check into a B&B or a hotel near Lake Superior. He would thumb through the channels, and I would flip through the attraction guide and begin planning our activities. I would be in search of romance. He would want to shop for antiques. I would be thrifty and want to hold my funds for one special thing. He would purchase a variety of things indiscriminately: mugs, hats, blankets, stones, filling his basket until it was full of stuff.

Vacation sleep is the most glorious. I slept until my bio-rhythms told me it was time to get up, not the usual insomnia I felt each night envisioning another day of recruitment work. I would always find him sitting up and enjoying an ancient movie he found on the classics channel. Undoubtedly someone would be hungry, so we'd turn to the Inn Keepers guide for assistance. I would dress in wrinkled khaki capris and soft soul sandals. We'd walk down the hall hand in hand, slowly, because we certainly were in no hurry. Always, we found ourselves near large water: the St. Croix, Lake Superior, Lake Michigan. Tourist towns in the northern Midwest sprout near water, giving cooler temps and the feeling of being away from the six-lane highways that lead us into and out of the commonplaceness of suburbia. I would have great expectations knowing there would be no distractions, at least for a few days. I would expect him to look in my eyes and see something different, something more than what he saw yesterday, or the days, months, and years before that. Summer is the season we bask in. My winter skin was near-supple again. Why not try again? So, I would try and try and try.

• • •

But there was no B&B that summer. Greg was busy working. At first, I barely noticed his absence. The closest we came was one disastrous weekend at Mary and John's cabin. We were one of four couples, and I had hoped no one could hear our angry whispers at night. He didn't want to be away at the cabin. He needed to be at work "adding value to the company." The company was in the local news. Everyone knew the former cash cow was going bankrupt. It was just a matter of time before his job would be lost, along with the hundreds of others that had gone before his. He said that, while others sat conspicuously at their desks eagerly surfing the net for alternative employment options, he was still trying to distinguish himself as long as he could, in order to hold onto his job for as long as he could.

That sorry weekend at the cabin, we went to bed angry and woke up angry. I awoke and found him sitting at the foot of the bed with his hands gripping the edge of the mattress. "Good morning," I said. He said nothing, and I knew that it was going to be anything but a good morning.

"I have never forgiven you for stripping away my rightful place as the head of our household. God's plan was that I was supposed to be the head, and you took that away from me."

I said nothing. He left our room and I let a cold tear run across the bridge of my nose, my body curled in bed and unable to move.

• • •

The drive home was quiet. We returned home and went back to our separate corners. He worked. I wrote. I danced. I dined. I waited to become a mother. I continued to possess hope. Hope belonged to me.

• • •

During adoption summer we were invited to what the professionals referred to as an adoption picnic, which sounded an awful lot like an adoption party, something I vowed never to do. But my social worker told me a boy I learned about from the website would be there. I was interested in adopting a six-year-old boy, and Andre was a six-year-old boy. The story attached to his picture said Andre and his older brother would not be adopted as a sibling set. The older brother was physically aggressive toward the younger, and it was in the younger boy's best interest to be adopted alone.

"We'll eat, play games, you'll be asked to volunteer for one or two of the functions at the picnic." The social worker wanted to make me see this was no big deal.

Volunteer, I thought. I could serve a purpose other than eyeballing children and making judgments about them.

"I would be happy to volunteer," I responded. I was then told we needed to come to a training session before we attended the picnic. Obviously this was more than a simple picnic with food and games if you had to be trained on how to behave before you went.

We were taught not to cause harm by being stupid. The day of the picnic, I recited the few rules I did remember. *Don't be a child hog. Get involved with activities. Invite children of different ages to participate in an activity. Don't walk in with any pre-conceived notions of who you may want to take home with you.* I hated that we were going to do this. The choice in this made it all feel horribly wrong. Adopted kids are told they should feel special because they were "chosen" by their parents, but what about all of those children who were not chosen, how should they feel? What magic word is used to help them make sense of their particular situation?

We did decide to play by the rules, though we hadn't a clue how nor when to apply them. I saw the little girl from the web, the curious looking one who appeared to be evaluating me as I stared at the photo. Even in person, her face wore an expression that said she knew all things good and evil. Greg and I walked beside her as we found our way to the registration table. She looked up at me with the same inquisitive expression from her photo. I smiled at her, but said nothing. "Are you a mom?" She asked me. I considered her question an awkwardly long time before answering. At these functions, you were either a social worker, a child looking for parents, or an adult looking for a child. I was an adult looking for a child, but not a mom. She wanted to know my story. Finally, the answer came. "No," was the best I could do at the time. Black boys were the last to be adopted. I felt this to be the only humane element of our choosing. A boy of six was what we decided. That was old enough to be considered less desirable, but young enough to still need hugs and kisses from his parents.

I saw Andre's older brother tossing a football straight up into the air and catching it. Most of the children present I remembered from the website, or the monthly mailer we received featuring new updates. There were seven hundred children in our county who were waiting to be adopted. Most of those children were not being presented on websites, mailings, or at adoption picnics. Why? I don't know. But the children who were there I had seen before, and knew a little something about most. I could point out the straight-A students. I knew who had ADHD, or attachment disorder, or post-traumatic stress from earlier abuses. I could point out the ones who experienced what they call an adoption disruption. That is when a child was placed with a family for adoption and the family changed their minds after the child was placed with them. Or the social workers changed their minds about the family. We were told that it was often the family deciding that they couldn't handle the challenges of raising the child. They would sometimes try for a month, or several months, believing they could find a way to have a relationship with the child, but they discovered the child refused to attach to them. The county would put them back on the websites, back on display. "I could be a good kid, if someone would give me a chance." These were the words written in the bio of one boy who experienced a disruption. I inquired about him, although he was older than six now, nearly thirteen. There was hesitation from the social worker as she shared with me his challenges, which included physical aggression. I did not inquire further.

• • •

There was a gathering of teenagers far off into their pack, as teenagers often traveled, seemingly unfazed by the seeking adults swooning nearby. I imagined by this point they would be cynical as each day brought them closer to their next birthday, closer to the date of emancipation. I suppose emancipation was supposed to be their magic word, but it simply meant they would turn eighteen and be forever without a family, at least in the sense of having a mom or a dad. When they married, who would sit on their side of the church? When babies are born, who would their children call "Grandma"? When they traveled to distant parts, what would be the home they returned to?

After marriage, I had emancipated myself from my birth family. I knew to a fraction of a degree what it was like not to have the safety net of parents.

I don't know why I felt something of an orphan since leaving Farragut for college. It wasn't that my family disowned me or pushed me away. It was just that I chose to remove myself from their midst. I was still trying to leave my past behind, still trying to recreate another me, still acting as if that were possible. I never fought with my husband about whose family we would spend holidays with. It was always Greg's. When I left home, my family seemed to be scattered like dust particles you could only see at the brightest hour of the day. You try to catch the mote in your hands and only manage to disturb the dust, but never hold it. I did not realize that, during all the years I would be away, my family would develop a certain kind of cohesion. They would be a family without me.

But there I was, so many miles away and trying to create a family of my own. We were the quiet Carters from the northwest metro, and we were being instructed to "mix" with as many youth as possible. "Don't stand there and watch the children. That will only make them feel like they're on display," said one social worker we had never met prior to this event as she approached us to find out more about us. We told her we wanted to meet Andre.

"Yes, I saw him just a second ago." She took a couple of steps back, scanning the field. "I see him. Follow me." Timidly, we followed the marching social worker, a few paces behind her.

"Hi, Andre, this is Greg and Sherrie Carter. They wanted to play with you for a bit. Is that all right?" I bent down to shake his hand.

"Hello. What have you been up to today?"

Andre shrugged.

"How about a game of horseshoes?"

"I don't care."

I didn't remember six-year-olds being so small. His legs and arms looked like drumsticks. I remember attempting to instruct him on how to throw a horseshoe.

"You don't want to toss it like a Frisbee but like this, underhanded . . . gentle." The six-year-old quickly grew bored with us and was soon off alone again to play in the dirt.

I was nervous about everything about that day, including my appearance. I told Greg what I wanted him to wear. "Don't wear beige. It's not friendly. No. Gray is even worse. Wear blue. Blue is a good color on you." I wore a bright yellow top. My clothing did not make me the kid magnet I hoped it would. I could have been wearing a clown costume and it wouldn't have made any bit of difference. I was serious, and nervous, and weird, and boring, and stupid. Stupid, stupid, stupid.

Before the three-legged race, I took my partner to the side and gave an extemporaneous coaching session. "The key to winning is team work. We need to move like one person. Let's count together. one . . . two . . . one . . . two." Our outer legs moved on one and our shared leg moved on two. "We got the rhythm," I said as we practiced off to the side. The big payoff was a first place blue ribbon. My partner was thrilled. I was relieved. Feeling confident about our picnic game ability, we tried the balloon toss. My eight-year-old partner fell to the ground in tears when the balloon burst on the first toss.

The picnic was over four hours after it started. Greg and I barely partook in the brats and beans served that day, and we developed an incredible appetite. Afterwards, driving to a nearby restaurant, I sat quiet and still. Greg was chatty. I congratulated him on being so wonderful with the kids that day. He followed the rules. He engaged many children of several different ages. He volunteered to move heavy stuff. He even hung out with the teens. And somehow he found a way to scale the wall with Andre and experience a two-way conversation. Our whole afternoon, I had admired him from a distance. He did look good in his blue shirt. He was one of the few black men in attendance. I remember feeling that day that he was a good man and loving him for it.

We ordered a hearty meal at the steakhouse. Everything felt heavy, the glass, and the silverware. I dropped my fork and realized my hands felt weak and were shaking. "Look at my hands," I said to him and began to cry.

• • •

That evening, I was sitting home alone. Alone again because Greg was off to the office, or so I thought. That night alone, I discovered the very best feature to our home that was not pointed out by the former lady of the house who had dearly loved our house. I heard the first boom and wondered if the judgment day had come upon us before I could become a mom. I heard the boom again and ran to the window. It wasn't judgment day. It was the last night of Earl Brown days, our community celebration. I could not get a good view out of my window, so I went to our child's room, or the room that would belong to our child, if he ever arrived. Everything made sense, and I was delighted to the point of giddiness. "What a gift this will be to our child growing up in this small room," I thought. Each year they would be given a fireworks show, so close and so big that he would think it was just for him. I thanked God that evening for the day and for the perfect house.

10

THREE YEARS AFTER becoming a mother, I left Greg and what I thought was the perfect house. I took on the role of single mother, hoping one day my new ideal of one mom per child would come to pass, when Madison and I would cohabitate, co-shop, co-clean, co-pay bills, co-run up to school when shit goes down with the kids. Then, we'd fall into the same bed at night after a brutal day of childrearing, and wake up side-by-side ready to do it all over again. Sounded like a good old time to me, and I assumed that day would come eventually.

I have always been in love with old structures, buildings made at a time before people lived in boxy houses void of craftsmanship. Who didn't appreciate large urban trees that provide shade to those historic dwellings? Who didn't love sidewalks often not found in many suburban neighborhoods in the Twin Cities? It made me think of some of the neighborhoods in Brooklyn, the ones that I daydreamt about decades ago. JB and Jodi would be raised in a heavily democratic town with a small liberal arts college on every corner.

In the meantime, the kids and I moved to our first apartment in St. Paul. It was not a charming little place. It was cold. We kept hazardous electric heaters blowing throughout the night. Like my childhood apartment back in Brooklyn, my new apartment in Saint Paul was infested with mice. If they were looking for a warm place to wait out the Minnesota winter, they were in the wrong place. However, that didn't stop them from coming. The walls in our new place were so thin, it sounded like the chatter and drunken fights of our neighbors were in our own unit. The carcass of a dead bat rotted in the courtyard amid shattered glass. The street outside was busy with traffic, and cheap windowpanes made it easy to hear the slurred speech of men making their way south from the bar a few blocks north of us. Still, I tried to love Saint Paul. It held a promise within. It was the city where Madison lived. First, I would have to establish myself independently. Then, Madison, JB, Jodi, and I would live as one family. That was my hope.

On the first day of first grade, I sat with the twins under cafeteria lights. JB ate his corn flakes out of a paper bowl. Jodi was not hungry, which was unusual.

"You're both going to have a great first day. I can't wait to hear all about it." I held both of them in my arms.

Jodi cried, "Don't leave me, Mommy. Pleeeease . . ."

"Honey, you're going to be fine. You're going to have so much fun."

She cried harder and louder. JB looked a little nervous, but appeared to be ready to take on the day.

I tried to reassure the six-year-olds they could trust me. I knew what I was doing. We were more than capable of making the transition. We were strong. We were resilient. We were not victims. We left the house on Thurber Road, and life would only get better.

Jodi fastened herself to me like a belt pulled too tight, with no give between us. I was anxious about being late for work.

"I'll take her." A staff member rescued me, pulling Jodi away as she cried.

Jodi noodled to the ground as I headed for the door.

I hurried out of the building, weeping, and told myself that it was the first day. It was just another first day, one in a long line of many first days to come. That was not the first time Jodi unraveled at school, and it wasn't likely to be the last. It had started in pre-school.

Jodi started falling out when I dropped her off in the morning. By that time, she seemed to change her mind about where she wanted to be. Instead of not wanting to be at preschool, she wanted to spend the day with me. The shift signified she was becoming attached. She was beginning to see me as her mommy.

Soon after Jodi started preschool, she began biting, kicking and insulting the teachers, and knocking over toys and garbage cans. In her mind, they were all poopy-heads. I showed up in the middle of the day. I hugged and kissed her. I tried to let her know she was safe, but my words were meaningless, just like the day they started first grade at their new school. In first grade, the same behaviors persisted, chairs and bookshelves pushed to the ground by the six-year-old. She had a habit of running out of the classroom with no particular destination in mind. Once, she tried to climb out of the first-floor window. Later, in elementary school, Jodi was still getting suspended for similar acts—school furniture her first target. Her language graduated from "poopy-head" to "bitch," "nigger," and "fuck you!" "Shut the fuck up, bitch!" She might yell on a day when she was well past her wall of tolerance. She kicked, punched, slapped, and scratched at her teachers' faces, drawing blood.

JB, who was once the quiet child, found his voice. He would demand to be heard by speaking incessantly, arguing his point of view until I finally stated the decision had been made and he needed to live with it. He discovered his own wall of tolerance. JB used to watch quietly the commotion when his sister came undone, and I knew he unraveled when he told an afterschool staff to "Shut the fuck up!" I remember my mantra when leaving Thurber Road. *We are resilient. Things could only get better.*

JB, once the zen, evangelist child, found the combination to his angry box. Once it was unlocked, I could not shut it. Once, he was so angry at a girl with physical disabilities in his class who wore a helmet to protect her head from a potential fall, he swiped her helmet from the table and ran out of the classroom. If that wasn't bad enough, he went to the boys' bathroom, dropped the helmet in a toilet and peed in it.

The social worker at school suggested JB and Jodi attend a "friendship group" at school for children who were struggling with their parents' breakups.

Madison was rightfully anxious about the slow pace of the divorce process. Madison and I had declared our love for one another about six weeks after that day at the pizzeria and about two weeks after our first, "official" date. Still, Madison said she would not kiss me until my divorce was final. I wore her down and continued to promise my mind, body, spirit, time, and resources no longer belonged to Greg and my conscience was clear. I was free to love again. After some convincing, she granted me her lips. However, we would not do much more than that until the state of Minnesota also agreed I was a liberated woman.

She wondered why I continued to talk to Greg on the phone. Why I tried to be a friend and encourage him in his new relationship. I tried to explain I liked the latest woman in his life. She was good to JB and Jodi. I still needed Greg to be okay. I believed a better Greg meant a better father for JB and Jodi, and a better JB and Jodi meant a better me. I was not going to be fine if the kids weren't fine. Dr. Phil said a mother is only as happy as her least happy child. Genetically, we were not tied. There was no umbilical cord that needed to be cut, but we were nonetheless connected—spiritually, emotionally, and legally, they were mine.

Madison felt resentment from the kids. Was she the reason for their parents' breakup? They never asked me this question. But their behavior felt like giveaways.

"Don't touch my sweatshirt. It's very special to me," Jodi said to Madison. "My dad gave that to me."

"Leave if you want to," JB once said to Madison.

Madison often had to engage with angry children, and the woman she loved seemed to be taking her sweet time in ending the marriage she claimed not to want. I'm sure she had to ask herself more than once, "Just what am I getting out of this deal?"

"You know I want out, but my hands are kind of full here." In the first few months after leaving Thurber Road, I was being called to school multiple times a week. Jodi was physically aggressive with staff. JB was stealing from his classmates.

Greg and I blamed each other.

"You did this!"

"Me! You have completely lost touch with reality."

I was losing Madison. She tried to end it a couple of times. Once, she cited biblical reason, saying, "This is wrong. I feel wrong." Later, the situation was too chaotic.

My love valued safety and security. I realized this soon after we started spending time together. Before leaving her car, she held the automatic buttons to her windows and counted to ten. She did this four times until she was certain her closed windows were actually closed. Then, she jiggled the gearshift three times. Before leaving the house she checked the stove, "Off, off, off, off, off." After locking the door to her apartment, she twisted the knob three times. When she entered her apartment after being out, she checked windows and closets, and looked underneath her bed. I on the other hand, had opposite issues. I used to forget to pay bills because it would just slip my mind. I would forget to cash a tax refund check because I neglected to open my mail. My voicemail was always full. I would forget to renew my license plate tabs until I was reminded by the police officer who had just pulled me over. When JB and Jodi were diagnosed with ADHD, I learned I had the same condition. I had an inability to focus. Having too many things to do easily overwhelmed me, which is why parenting alone felt like a death sentence.

There were times when we could experience glimpses of almost normal.

The everyday Jodi was good with tykes. She thought they were "sooo cuuute" even when they were out of control, defiant little snots. She could have been an old lady already the way she complained about her body aches—her bad knee, her sore ankle, and her stiff back. Who knew if she was just imitating the grunts and groans of her worn-out mother, the fat dancer with arthritis in both her knees?

JB inherited my proclivity for caution. On most days, I appreciated his willingness to declare "I'm gonna tell Mom on you!" It kept Jodi out of trouble when she was tempted to watch R-rated horror movies on Netflix, or cross the forbidden, high-traffic street that separated them from their preferred playground. Jodi was daring, and JB was the tattler. Together, they could be the perfect blend of strengths and weaknesses for an adventurous childhood.

At times, it appeared we were the typical dysfunctional family.

"No! I don't want you to sit by me!" Jodi yelled at her brother.

"But I wanted to sit here. I already set my plate down."

"But I want Madison to sit by me!"

"How do we promote peace in our home?" Again, I had to ask Jodi and JB that question. My method of parenting usually involved asking questions and getting them to think about how our behaviors might be perceived by others.

"Well, it's his fault. He's always bothering me!"

"Okay. Let me try this again. How can we promote peace in our home?"

"How is it my fault?" JB completely ignored my question. "This is why I should just kill myself! Maybe Jodi will be happy then!"

"Guys. This isn't constructive. This isn't how we promote peace. There should be no talk of killing, not ourselves or anyone else.

"Yeah. You're so dramatic, Jabori."

"Well, you would be dramatic too if you had a sister like you!"

"Okay—Wait a minute both of you. I'm asking you to think about what each of us can do as individuals to create an atmosphere of acceptance and love. If everyone is only concerned about making sure their own needs are met, there's going to be a lot to fight about. We're going to be in constant battle. Our home should be a place of refuge."

"Listen to your mother." Madison always supported me. Her presence kept me centered like nothing else could.

"Am I making any sense?" I asked Madison.

"You make perfect sense, baby."

"Thank you," I leaned over for a kiss, and she met me halfway.

"You make sense, Mommy. But I would have more peace if JB wasn't so annoying."

"If I'm annoying, you're mean and rude and that's worse!"

"Okay . . . let's talk about this more later. You're not ready to learn from me right now. Maybe you'll both have to learn things the hard way. Maybe, as your mother, I just need to accept that."

Every parent wishes their children would not have to suffer too much in order to learn life's lessons. We wish we could learn it all for them, so they wouldn't have to undergo too much trauma or drama before they finally learn to crave peace. There was a time when bullshit drama was all I knew. I learned enough lessons for ten lifetimes. I learned enough to do a better job at walking a little more wisely in the world. I want them to know that kindness begat kindness and love magnified love. Do you have to be four decades old in order to really be able to embrace this extraordinarily simple idea?

Monsters

My life is lived in coalescence
with other younger lives.

Perfect Silence speaks
and beckons my focus upon its face
above ground,
above trees that imitate shadows

to where bright speckles
share space among
the dark and endless deep

Beyond this terrestrial milieu
Perfect Solitude sends its greeting.
Tells me not be afraid of somersaulting
like weightless debris without objective

With nothing to obtain and
nothing to maintain. I will be
glad to know there are
no translations for words
like *mommy.*

Above trees that imitate monsters,
I am Perfectly Forsaken.
Free from ones who bicker
and demand I punish their sibling.

•••

Filling out the forms to dissolve my marriage, I tried to be "fair." I petitioned for joint custody. If we had joint custody, Greg would be less likely to be required to pay child support. I requested we both keep the cars that we drove—he should keep the Oldsmobile that was already paid off, and I keep the blue station wagon, which was a year from being paid off. I had no interest in the house on Thurber Road. I could never afford the mortgage alone, and neither could Greg after he lost his job.

Before leaving the house on Thurber Road, I had called Sophia, Greg's former girlfriend.

"You'll never guess who this is."

"I know who this is," she answered.

"You might think I'm crazy, but I wanted to let you know I'm leaving Greg."

"Good. I'm glad for you."

"I also wanted you to know he's still in love with you."

"I know. I told him to stop sending me gifts. I don't want anything to do with him."

"Are you sure?" I asked.

"I left Minnesota. I'm going to remarry my former husband."

"Really?"

"Really. When I was with Greg, I became a different person. I never thought I'd be in a situation like that—the other woman."

"I understand."

"I'm glad you're leaving Greg. He needs to suffer for what he did to you."

I didn't need Greg to suffer. In fact, I needed Greg to be at peace. I needed Greg to be well, so he could be a good father to JB and Jodi. Deepak Chopkra said, "The best way to get rid of your enemy is to increase their capacity for happiness." I didn't want

Greg to be my enemy, and the truth of the matter was I was afraid to parent alone. I needed the other half of the parenting team to be able to share the load. However, though I had tried, I was unsuccessful at increasing Greg's happiness. Sophia was not interested. Greg's rage continued.

I assumed Madison would save me from the plight of single-parenthood. She was going to be the cool and funny stepparent who the kids would come to instead of me because she would be the pushover. That was how I imagined it, but I couldn't wish that life into existence.

One break-up was my doing. I was angry Madison didn't catch my vision, which was for us to co-parent together and live under one roof. Madison was the cure for my chronic loneliness, beginning with my family of origin and our lack of togetherness, to the solitary living I participated in during college, to eighteen years of being deeply alone with Greg because I always had the sense he'd rather be somewhere else, with someone else. Madison was a part of my life. She was kind to me, but having her on a part-time basis was painful. I worked so hard to make it happen. I left Greg. I moved into a rodent-infested, tiny fourplex and froze all winter long. I started JB and Jodi at a new school. Both kids were falling apart, and I didn't know how to put them back together. I was still subject to Greg's verbal onslaughts. Sometimes, he would belittle me or criticize my parenting. Other times, he would threaten to harm me just as he had done for the eighteen years we were together. Sometimes I believed him when he told me I didn't know how to parent. I questioned all the choices I had made up until then. Madison said I was more than capable of pulling through. However, I did not see how I was going to do that alone. Alone was for writing or listening to my favorite music. Alone was for sitting on a bench and resting one's body and spirit under a tree without interference from other voices. Alone was for restorative time, not for raising broken children, not for recovering from a lifetime of feeling alone.

While Madison was away visiting family, I left a voicemail on her cell phone because she always kept her phone off during the day, which meant she remained unavailable until she was ready to talk to me. "It's over," I said. However, in less than twenty-four hours I had changed my mind.

"I don't know what came over me. Please forgive me."

"I can forgive you in time," she said.

"And then, can we forget this ever happened? It was a mistake."

"I will honor your wishes, if you don't want to be with me."

"But I do want to be with you."

"But, I think you were right. This isn't working."

Begging was not beneath me. "It was an impulsive and stupid thing to do. You broke up with me twice, and I took you back right away. I forgave you. Why can't you forgive me?"

"I said I will forgive you in time."

For weeks, I begged Madison to take me back. It was a nightly ritual.

"Please take me back."

"I can't."

"Why?"

"Because I can't." Madison agreed to be my friend, but she refused to see me. She stayed in Milwaukee for a full month while classes were not in session and she did not have to teach.

I was sick with missing Madison. After two weeks had gone by, I tried to accept that our break-up was final. In doing so, I needed to somehow define my sexuality without a mate. I learned that a local women's center facilitated a support group for women coming out later in life. Coming out later in life meant a woman who had had significant relationships with men. Before falling in love with

Madison, I spent eighteen years with the man I met in college. In high school, I dated only boys. I felt a need to explain all this to myself and to others who knew me before Madison. Was this sexuality always a part of me, or was it something new? One person surmised my attraction for Madison had little to do with my sexuality and more to do with Madison. She would appeal to most anyone, male or female, because she was funny, kind, and worked hard. Because of Madison's gender non-conforming presentation, one might argue I was still attracted to masculinity. Appearance had very little to do with heart. Her outward presentation did not hide her woman's soul. I really didn't believe I would feel differently if she wore pumps instead of construction boots.

At the start of the spring semester, after a month's separation, Madison and I saw each other at an on-campus meeting. She smiled at me the way she did before we broke up.

"You look good."

"I missed you," I said.

"I missed you, too."

That evening, when I called Madison with the ritual request to take me back, she said yes.

Over the next months, I went to the same women's center to seek free legal advice in dissolving my marriage. I filed more paperwork. I showed up for the scheduled divorce hearing, and waited anxiously outside of the courtroom for the proceedings to begin. Inside, a man with white shoulder-length hair sat on his bench, a young clerk next to him. I took my seat and waited for Greg to enter. He never did. The judge wanted to be sure Greg received notification, and rescheduled our hearing.

Months later, I arrived at the courthouse again. I waited anxiously to be called into the courtroom. Again, Greg did not show.

For the third time, I arrived at the Ramsey County Courthouse, wondering if Greg would come.

The judge explained that he received word from Greg Carter. He was unable to attend the proceedings because he had moved out of state. However, he had written a letter to the judge. The judge did not read the entire letter, but he did read the part conveying that my desire to divorce stemmed from Greg losing his job.

It took another six months of going to and from the courthouse before my divorce was officially granted by a judge in Ramsey County. The day I received my divorce decree in the mail, I hurried to the copy center. I wanted to present Madison with evidence that my life with Greg was officially done. I continued to utter the words, "It is finally done. It's done, done, done."

Madison's reaction was better than I imagined. We laughed and held each other. It was evidence I was completely committed to our future. We were free to be together. We could draw up the plans. Decide where we would live and when we would move. I staged a campaign for why it only made sense we live together. Of course, the one problem was the plan only made sense to me.

Living with children meant living in a constant state of disorder. Living with children who did not trust adults was living in a constant mode of fight or flight—will I live in conflict mode, or will I spend every day wishing I could be somewhere else? These were Madison's thoughts.

I asked myself whether she loved me enough to find a way to make it work. Her answer remained the same. She loved me too much to move in with us and become a family of four. She knew it would not work. She knew she would end up resenting me for it.

I feared I would resent her for not agreeing to move in with me. Had we come to an impasse? I read dreadful statistics to her regarding the fate of single mothers. I decided to take on these new demands although I was living the life of one of those profoundly challenged single mothers I read about in a women's magazine who have a seventy percent greater chance of dying an early death than mothers with full-time partners. Every moment of the day is accounted for, and spending time in a state of stillness is simply impossible when you know you forgot to pick up your daughter's medication at the drug store and it's nearly the kids' bedtime. You are assisting your son as he meticulously works on his school project due the next day and there isn't a stitch of clean underwear in the house. So, you debate. Do you grab the kids, pick up the meds, and purchase new underwear to get us through the rest of the week even though it's a total waste of money? Money is already stretched into mesh. It could, however, save you a little energy. After all, you're exhausted and you still need to write something for the writer's workshop scheduled for the next evening. Shucks, you then remember you forgot to confirm with the thirteen-year-old babysitter if she was still available to watch your kids. You'll have to get off work earlier, pick up the babysitter on the other side of the river, and make sure you have cash on hand to pay the pizza delivery guy. You realize this is an insane way to live. Your children are a year behind in their dental appointments, and you continue to forget to schedule that mammogram for yourself as your doctor suggested.

• • •

Madison spent her childhood focusing on her goal to get accepted into a good college. Once in college, her new goal was to be accepted into a PhD program. Once in the PhD program, her new goal became finish her dissertation and graduate. Close to graduation, it was to be hired into a tenure track position. Then, be granted tenure. Then, publish her first book. Then, increase her speaking engagements and become the public sociologist she always wanted to be. Throughout her life, Madison stayed on task, achieving one long-term goal after another.

She never thought she would fall in love with a mother. She imagined meeting someone who actually had time for her. She and this woman would have time alone in order to determine if they were compatible. They would get to know each other over quiet meals and conversations about the state of humankind and not be interrupted by six-year-olds fighting for their mother's attention. Date nights would not include animated movies with a couple rounds of Candyland. Dating a woman with children meant determining if she and the children were also compatible. Could they co-exist peacefully, if not joyfully? What happens then, if the woman's children have behavioral issues due to past trauma? What happens when the mother's crying most nights because she received another call about one of her children disrupting class or being disrespectful toward their teachers, or because someone has been suspended and she'll have to miss a day at work? What happens when the woman had dreams and goals of her own and she's angry at the whole universe because she doesn't feel she has the time or the energy to bring her dreams into reality?

11

MADISON AND I MET for lunch at the pizzeria, the day she told me she needed me to finish my book. Our lives changed in an instant. When we met, she wanted to be without romantic attachment in order to do God's work. Later I learned her upbringing was still present in her psyche. She wasn't confident her God would bless a same-sex relationship. She wondered what she had gotten herself into. Not only was she falling for a woman, again, she was falling for a woman legally married to a man.

In my years of knowing her, I only heard Madison swear once. Slow traffic halted as the light changed from yellow to red. We were chatting about whether or not our good friend would enjoy the gift we just purchased for her in celebration of her tenure and promotion. Just before the light turned green, some guy slammed hard into the back of her car.

Quietly, she barely uttered, "Shit, not again." It hadn't been more than a month since she got her car out of the auto-body shop after the last preoccupied driver rear-ended her.

I found relief in knowing she was capable of using four-letter words, if only under life-threatening circumstances. A definite guide governed Madison's life. Her grandmother illuminated her ecosphere in Milwaukee public housing. Madison came to love the Jesus her grandmother first taught her to love, although she expressed it somewhat differently in her adult life. She was raised in a charismatic church, and although she would say she had not been given the gift to speak in tongues, she did believe the gift existed. Her grandmother's Jesus taught her to live an honest life and never be too big to ask for God's direction or forgiveness.

Not only was Madison careful about the language she used, she didn't drink, and she respected her "elders" like no one I had ever known in the northern states—lots of "yes, ma'ams" and "no, sirs." She would not eat without offering thanks to God, and she wouldn't leave the house until she had read her Bible and allowed its message to take shape in her spirit. She was committed to Sunday morning service and good things were always received as a blessing. Luck had nothing to do with it. After finishing graduate school and purchasing her first car, she named it G.G.—God's Gift. Madison's desire to live a structured and wholesome life came honestly. It was part of her upbringing. I think it was the way she survived her childhood struggle. I survived by finding freedom through my imagination. She survived by creating order in her physical surroundings.

When Madison and I met, I was a Sunday school teacher. However, when I stopped attending church regularly, she gave me wake-up calls on Sunday morning.

"Going to church today?" she'd asked.

"Not today," I sometimes answered.

Sometimes she accepted my answer. Other times, she would suggest I needed to be recharged. "You need to feed your soul, dear."

"Don't worry, honey. I'll listen to Krista Tippet on public radio."

"Okay, dear . . ." she'd answer, usually sounding as if she wanted to say more, but knowing how hard it had been to get through to me regarding church matters.

"I think I might convert to Buddhism, anyway. Do you think there are Buddhist who also believe in Jesus?"

"Probably. I don't know much about it."

"I don't either, but I plan to look into it."

"When do you think you will look into?"

"Eventually, when the spirit so moves me."

"Okay, dear. But at least read the devotions I gave you."

"Okay, honey. Enjoy service."

"Love you, dear."

"Love you too, honey." I repositioned myself and attempted to rediscover my groove. I thanked God for my sweetie and drifted off to sleep.

•••

Once, the "Battle Hymn of the Republic" played in my third ear, though it was more faint those days than when my pursuit of motherhood first began. I recalled thirty, the blessed assurance, the horn section, once fully occupying the space around me, now whispered through my translucence. At that point, I was thin—physically, I was thinner, yes. But what I mean to say is that it was as if sound, light, and other forms of energy must not have taken hold, because there was very little substance to hold onto, just a meshing of delicate threads pulling apart, one by one.

Even as I snapped, the belief was there that life could be as spectacular as a light-show of celestial bodies. . . . Sometimes, I called it hope, called it faith, called it optimism, even as I threw the telephone down with elation whizzing through me as I gawked at the dismembered parts scattered across the ugly linoleum. Thrilled at what had been annihilated—smashed to bits—dead for sure, and for one abbreviated moment, I felt powerful. Another broken item, cheap enough to replace.

Even in the midst of self-battery, a fool-hearted belief was there. The beatings started the night I first learned there was a very tall and shapely woman named Sophia in Greg's life. It started with pounding my fist onto the basement floor, pounding my chest, pounding my head, over and over. It continued during the repair period, which was supposed to be our time of marital recovery . . . when we were prescribed a regimen of counseling sessions and therapeutic dating by our marriage and family therapist. During these dates, I felt Greg's absence most of all. Sometimes he would look as if boredom had taken its toll on his weary soul. I would stare at him and count how long before he noticed I was staring at him. Sometimes he never noticed. I would be the one to notice things, notice everything, like the nervous fluttering of the eyelids when he lied. "You're not still seeing her?" I asked. "No, Sherrie, I'm not." It was our night, and we were having dinner at Tony Roma's. One of those nights I would go through the trouble of hiring a babysitter, and getting myself dressed in form-fitting clothes and uncomfortable shoes, when I noticed, as I had noticed many times before, that he was not wearing his wedding ring. He lost it, he said. This would be the third of four wedding rings purchased during the duration of our marriage. Sometimes, I would try to explain, as best as I could, what the betrayal felt like. I would say if felt like a death, like someone had died. But no one had died, and if this was the worst thing I'd ever gone though, he would say my life was pretty good. Still I continued to beg for his empathy, and there usually was none. I begged for his honesty, and there was little of that as well. I could tell when he was missing her most intensely by his effort to demolish me with his words, "fat and ugly . . . bitch . . . weak . . . lousy in bed," slinging any horrible thing that came to mind. I watched him mourn the loss of the baby Sophia miscarried, while I mourned the fact that he almost had a child with another woman. Then he said I was selfish and only cared about myself.

• • •

Sometimes, not every time, but a few times there were too many volatile forces happening at the same time—PMS, my poorly cooked dinner, the bowl of spaghetti JB dumped onto the carpet. Combine these occurrences with sleep deprivation and the fact I had mostly given up food. Combine this with the fact I was still adjusting to the task of being a mother, and my first job was to give them whatever they needed. Combine this with the fact I still had career goals and an overwhelming desire to write, but mostly could not write because too many obstacles stood in the way of free-flowing thoughts. I had no words. I was a writer with no words and a mother with no love. Behind closed doors, I would try to protect Jodi and JB from me, pound on myself, muffle my sobbing, smack my own face to get a fucking grip, releasing the anger against myself, because there wasn't anyplace else to put it. There was no place to lay it down, so I laid it on myself as hard as I could. But even within these moments, I could hear the faint music and I'd see the dim lights above when I just took a moment to breathe. I would be reminded of what life could be, what life is for those who choose it. Caving out of exhaustion, I would whimper until asleep.

• • •

Upon waking . . .

Everyone lying facedown on the floor must say to themselves in that moment there has to be a better way. At the moment, I think I knew I had to be there, groveling and full of self-pity, outside of that holy presence, outside of joy, and even outside of my mind. Upon waking, I would continue my search toward better.

I never really did well with authority. I have always been terribly compliant with rules and regulations, I just never felt fully at ease with the rulers or the regulators. The story of God had been viewed through the eyes of men. I had grown weary of God the Father. I wanted to know what Mother God would have me know. I considered the slave ship named Jesus, captained by Christian men of the cloth, and considered all of the ways Christianity had been used as a tool for evil and was ready to give the whole business up. But despite my doubts, questions, and fears, when I was in need of spiritual healing, it was the Bible I opened, the Church doors I entered, and Jesus' name I spoke.

So, in phases, I chose to seek first the kingdom of heaven, devouring every scriptural text read or spoken like nuggets, whole and delectable. "Be imitators of God, therefore as dearly loved children and live a life of joy." So SHe was the author of love, and look at this, SHe wanted me to live a life of joy. If I was truly going to immerse myself in spiritual matters in that way, I had to stop thinking about the followers who denied the part of Her that is all women.

In my early twenties, I married Greg Carter and we lived a church-going existence. The deity, the love, the belief in God was supposed to become the unifying belief in our home. We were both supposed to work to shed our former selves to become reborn in the new image. For me, the hope of God's love drew me to Jesus, though I had been drawn before and strayed away. I embraced what I believed to be our universal solvent to all our past and future ailments. I believed what it said in Proverbs, "Those who plan for what is good, find love and faithfulness." It was like saying whatever you're looking for, you're bound to find it. The lesson was to look for good.

I wanted to believe God knew me well and could translate my moans into fully articulate sentences. Jeremiah 1:5 says, "The word of the Lord came to me saying, before I formed you in the womb, I knew you. Before you were born I set you apart." In my new life I wanted to learn to balance the idea that we were great and small all at the same time, but ultimately, there was someone else who was causing the earth to move.

Sometimes the beauty and the love I found through faith would change into something less beautiful and loving. We were in our early twenties and being molded in the image of something I wasn't quite sure about. My husband attended Promise Keeper events at the Metrodome, raised his hands, though he was not one to be that demonstrative, and sang praises to our great god in the sky who instructed my mortal husband to lord over me. Women could teach children and other women, but it was not our place to teach men, though deep down I believed there was so much they could learn from us. I could organize women's retreats and attempt to teach Bible stories to preschoolers, like that of Jacob and Esau, the twin boys who were two separate nations in their mother's womb (the elder would serve the younger), trying my best to understand why God would predetermine one child to be greater than his brother. "Our understanding is limited. My job is not to understand His ways. My job is to trust and obey. I believe. Help my disbelief." I repeated these phrases to myself in order not to get stuck in my questions. Eventually, my spirit advanced from questioning to rebelling (as is often the case with women, I was told) every time we were asked to turn to Ephesians 5:22 where Paul wrote, "Wives, submit to your husband as to the Lord." I knew the next twenty minutes would feel like twenty years because I had heard it all before. Of course, the husband was to love his wife as he loved his own body, as Christ loved the church. But, for the sake of order, God instructed husbands to be the head. There could only be one head.

I've always dreamt about leaving in the middle of a "submit" sermon. Instead, I sat there and allowed the muscles at the center of my stomach to contract. I would take deep breaths, but try not to let out too loud of a sigh. I would make my face go blank, so as not to give any indication of my displeasure. Though I contained myself, I still felt pretty sure this verse was not supposed to be used as a weapon against us. I would repress my insubordinate spirit, which understood rebellion was a natural consequence of oppression.

"Turn with me to Ephesians five, verse twenty-two," the pastor would say in his usual tranquil demeanor one more Sunday. Without any plan to do so, I was up out of my seat and running out of the sanctuary while letting out this enormous and horrible sound. Out of the church building, I ran in weighty flip-flops—wailing as I ran the three blocks of the quiet suburban neighborhood toward my car. The preacher's wife, my friend who I loved dearly like a beloved older sister, was right behind me, though I did not know it at first. A deacon was behind her. My husband, who licked these "submit" messages up as if they were as tasty as buttercream frosting, was behind the deacon. "I can't take it!" I repeated. "I can not take it!" Perhaps I had felt, for some reason, the whole world needed to know just how much I could not take it.

Later, I did the church-hopping thing, trying on many different styles. Once, I attended an inner city church by the name of Total Victory. I dressed the children and we all went. I just loved the name. "Total Victory." It was what I wanted. I tried to convince myself that, if I was going to be victorious, I had to live victoriously. I loved songs with those themes. "In the name of Jesus, we've got the Victory. In the name of Jesus, Satan will have to flee." It was an up-tempo, hand-clappin', feet stompin' type of song, as it should be when singing about Jesus. Like fans shouting "We Will Rock You" at a football game, it was designed to turn the doubters into believers. The kind of song that could give you a little more faith to believe just one more day.

I sat in Total Victory feeling less than victorious, my face wet with tears, my thin hands cold in the drafty old sanctuary. The church was unlike any I'd been to. The men's choir got up and did a Jesus version of the Temptations' song, "I've got sunshine on a cloudy day." Only it was, "I guess you say, what can make me feel this way . . . my God . . . my God . . . my God." The women were on their feet shouting. They had the falsetto, the baritone and everything. The preacher was unorthodox. No robe, which was a very contemporary thing to do, but also no suit and tie. Rather he was wearing a silk shirt and a thick gold chain and a gold watch I would have ordinarily considered ostentatious. It was all a little peculiar for the proper (acting) Baptist girl in me. The message focused on the lives of the lowly, the broken . . . and one by one they came to the altar—the woman fighting cancer, the woman who lost her home in a fire and now she and her children were homeless, the man who relapsed into drug addiction. They also came to praise the Divine's faithfulness. One man stood up to say that, after twenty years, he found his biological sister. They were separated as children and raised in the foster-care system. They were both healing from past abuses, but they were there to testify that "Our God is a good God!" He made his sister, who was sitting next to him, stand. She was weeping, and the whole church was up on their feet. Shouting! And me, quiet me, shouting with my hands raised in the air in agreement that our God was a good God!

I walked out with my head up, still in a state.

"How'd you like the church?" I asked the children. JB and Jodi agreed they liked it very much. They wanted to come back next Sunday.

"Mommy, why were you crying?" Jodi asked

"I'm getting healed, honey."

"You should have got knocked down," JB suggested.

"Yeah, Mommy, you should have got knocked down," Jodi agreed. Remnants of their charismatic past were still with them. Before I became their mother, my children had gone to church with their foster family, where people got "knocked down," spoke in tongues, and danced in the spirit.

I could have explained that Mommy was a lukewarm Baptist. Instead, I told them that I thought they were right. "I should have gotten knocked down."

Years later, I would fall in love with a devout Christian gay woman and learn there was a whole world of gay people for Christ. Yet, I found myself without a church, without a "religion" to call my own. I'd attended wonderful houses of worship, one in particular which was open and affirming and filled to the brim with loving people. I began to feel religion did not close the gap between me and God, but left me lost in the forest where I could not find my place. The further I moved from church, the closer I got to God. I finally came to understand what Marianne Williamson meant when she said, "my life became a prayer."

My coming together with Madison was precarious and uncertain. We were afraid much of the time. She was afraid I would find my way back to Greg or that JB and Jodi would never accept her. Our failed relationship would prove she had no business loving another woman. I was afraid of screwing up all of our lives because I wasn't up to the challenge of being in control of my own life. "You must be looking for a live-in babysitter," Madison declared one Sunday afternoon we talked on the phone. I almost dropped the phone. Words got stuck in my throat. At first, only tears came. Then, the realization that it was way past time for me to function fully and totally on my own directed the course of my own life. I fled my life with Greg because I was tired of him being in control. Still, I was terrified of being in control myself. At the same time, I would snap if I sensed a hint of control from Madison. "You're not paying my bills, so you don't get to tell me what to do." We were often suspicious of each other's motives. When the reality of our mess got too much, we ran from each other. We blamed each other. We did not hold tight enough, and we found ourselves alone in our individual dwelling spaces, trying to save ourselves from the other woman. Soon, one woman would reach back for the other. The other woman would grab on and hold tight until the next time we found ourselves in trouble, feeling insecure, feeling as if we were in this love alone. Although I had strayed away from my religious traditions, to some degree, many aspects would always be grounding forces for me, such as the idea that *there is no fear in love.* I was pretty sure that lesson I would take with me to the end of my days. We had to trust each other.

JB, Jodi and I would move for the second time without Madison. Our second home was a lovely duplex a hundred years old with beautiful built-ins and a tranquil garden in the backyard, thanks to my landlord and the neighbor who lived next door. I no longer needed to live by some fictional depiction of what it meant to live an admirable life. I knew exactly what it meant to live an admirable life. It meant living life in love and not fear. I wanted this for me, for Madison, for JB, and Jodi.

"If we want us to work, we will work," I told Madison. We both agreed we wanted to stay together. We had to stop being afraid of being hurt, and we had to love. Our new mantra became, "if we want it to work, it will work." Because our desire was mutual, there was nothing to fret over.

12

THE DAY MADISON AND I met for pizza, she looked into me and said, "I need you to finish your book," and I wondered what she saw in me. Madison was well regarded in her department, her university, and in the field of sociology. I was working for the numero uno vice-president because it was my first move back in the world of full-time work. After learning about Sophia, the second woman outside of our marriage Greg would love, I was broken and a new mother of twins. I could not find my way to recover from my hurt and raise children who were in desperate need of a parent who was well. Greg said he wanted to try, so I removed myself from work and stayed home with JB and Jodi.

I did what I thought I was supposed to do as a stay-at-home mom. I enrolled the kids in soccer. I baked cookies. I cleaned the house and took my husband's shoes in to be repaired. JB, Jodi, and I went to the library, the zoo, the park. I packed our lunches for the day in order to save money. I remained thin a while longer in order to try to fit an image I had in my mind of a stay-at-home mother. I was the single mother of hurting children trying to make the most of a disastrous relationship.

We carried on this way for three months until Greg needed to leave for a business trip to the Southwest. Later, I found out it wasn't a business trip to the Southwest but a lover's excursion to the Southeast, Miami Beach to be exact. He even brought home little Miami T-shirts for JB and Jodi. I tried to rip the T-shirts to shreds, and when I couldn't do that with my bare hands, I cut them up with a pair of scissors. After that, I began looking for immediate work. Nothing was more immediate than temporary work. You can apply today and start working tomorrow. I temped around for two years. Where was my personal strength? Still, I continued with school and eventually finished my capstone project and graduated from my MFA program.

It wasn't until the day, I met Madison for pizza, the day she held her hands out before her and said, "Sherrie, I need you to finish your book," that I knew I was ready to leave Greg. For the first two full years, my focus was the same, to get Madison to move in with me. It was when I was still the soft girl from the projects.

• • •

During my youth there were some girls considered *too* grown. Linda Johnson kissed her boyfriend, Ricardo, before they departed on separate school buses at the end of each day saying, "Good-bye, honey. I'll see you tomorrow." They were first-graders, and this was already a two-year relationship. Later, in junior high, there was the girl who went by the name *Lady.* More than a name, it was a title that might have been given to her because she was so grown. Perhaps it was because she almost looked like Billy Holiday with her thick, wavy hair pulled back into a tight bun. She sauntered around the schoolyard in mock fur and sling-back pumps with girls who could only wish they could be her.

Some of these too-grown girls were my friends, like Gwen, who my mother fiercely disapproved of because she did not care for women and girls who were excessively loud. My friendship with Gwen betrayed my mother's idea of what it meant to be female: sweet and demure, never wearing blue jeans unless it was a day set aside for scrubbing floors, never speaking loudly unless your children were getting on your very last nerve. My mother's femininity was expressed clumsily through my body, a purposeless collection of flopping bones. Gwen, however, was thick-boned, or what the dudes in our neighborhood referred to as healthy. Undoubtedly, she had the most sought after rump in Farragut Projects.

In Gwen's case, grown implied fresh-mouthed, or a lack of respect for authority and her elders. More specifically, her teachers. More specifically still, Ms. Chase, who was a nasty, nasty woman—you might even say evil—who today we would say was emotionally unstable and most definitely unfit for the work of educating minors. Her fifth-grade students were her victims, and I was among the most intimidated.

Not Gwen. She vowed to take Ms. Chase down if she had to, and Gwen would just be the woman to do it. I never doubted that.

My mother did sanction my friendship with Natasha, who was taught to be unobtrusive and use her best manners when she entered someone's home—don't sit unless you were offered a seat, don't even walk past the entryway unless you were invited to do so. Natasha was my dearest friend and became my hero after her fight with Melvina Green, the thumb-sucking girl who would have kicked my ass if I did not pretend we were friends. Melvina just stepped to Natasha on the wrong day. It was during music. We had a new teacher, who was even more clueless than the last one. She was the same woman who referred to us as "minorities," and Freeman Johnson corrected her by saying we were not minorities because blacks and Puerto Ricans stuck together, right? He held his hand out for Joey Ortega to give him five, which Joey wholeheartedly did. The rest of us cheered!

Anyway, I can't remember what in the world Melvina said in the first place. I just remember Natasha demanding Melvina to leave her alone: "I'm tired of your mess!" I was tired of her mess too, but it wasn't like I was going do to anything about it. My plan was to grow up and move the hell out of the projects in one piece.

"So watchchu gonna do about it," Melvina said with her chest out.

"Keep messin' with me, and I will show you," Natasha said. I tried to cool things down, telling Natasha to just forget about it. "Just ignore her," I whispered so Melvina could not hear me. Natasha was newer to our neighborhood and did not fully appreciate the dimensions of Melvina's psychosis.

I don't know who slung the word "bitch" first. But at that point, it was beyond anything I could handle. The room went silent. Kids started backing up in case furniture started flying. We'd seen it happen. Melvina broke the silence with a hard smack, turning Natasha's light-brown complexion red. In an instant, Natasha's arm was around Melvina's neck and down they went onto the floor as the bystanders screamed for bloodshed. Our music teacher ran out of the room for help. When it was over, Natasha was hailed the victor, and she would never have to worry about Melvina Green ever again. I would never have to worry about Melvina Green ever again either, simply because I was Natasha's best friend, the one who welcomed her to our classroom when she was the new girl, to our neighborhood, and to my family's apartment one day after school and told her it was okay to come in and sit down.

Along with shutting down a bully, Natasha did two other things faster than any of us—own a bra and begin her period. Natasha's life was accelerated into womanhood when her mother died when we were in the sixth grade. I still remember four of us girls—Natasha, Gwen, Patrice Atwood, and me—huddled closely, weeping together with our friend who we admired deeply. We cried like it was all of our mothers who left this world. Natasha became the woman of the house, cooking, cleaning, watching over those itty-bitty sisters she kept perfectly groomed like little dolls. She was left relatively unsupervised by her stepfather. Eventually, there was some pot use, and as the TV warnings announced, pot opens the door to cocaine. . . . Then, crack entered the neighborhood. Then, there were two babies born addicted to crack. Then, there were two babies taken away by the Bureau of Child Welfare. But before that, before any of that, Natasha was my girl . . . my truest companion. Between us there were no harsh words, no foul moods, no misunderstandings, no one-ups, no pretense, no hurt feelings that could sometimes happen between girls . . . no competition. Even when Matt Flores, the boy I pledged myself to in secret, paid more attention to her than he did me, I thought, *of course he loves her. If I were a boy, I would love her too.*

I was the soft kid trying to recognize my place within the world of women-like girls. I would sometimes hear a girl be referred to as "delightful." I was not that, or fast in the pants, or a tomboy, or precocious, or somethin' else . . . as in "boy, she is somethin' else." I might have been something other, but I was never somethin' else. I'd worn glasses since the second grade and lacked the aptitude to get into too much trouble. Someone else set the rules and I followed them, like the time Jacqueline Long came up with the idea to sneak out of the schoolyard and steal cheese doodles from the corner bodega. I stole the cheese doodles, but Jackie ate them all, every last one. Never once had any adult looked at me to say, "You better know your place, young lady." No one ever said, "This girl is too damn grown for her own good."

• • •

At thirty-eight, I was still terrified, but considered the possibility that acceptance of my status as a single mother would be good for me. I could raise my children and achieve a few goals along the way, all with the ultimate goal of finishing my book.

I had to roll away the stone that blocked my view from my possibilities. It started with a job change. I stopped at the perfect job description.

> The program director will help students engage in this central question: *"How do I weave together my need to make a living with my need to live a fulfilling life?"*

The posting called for someone with a warm personality. *Really?* I thought. *My soft can be useful.* I had never seen that requirement written in a job description. I would encourage students to live within their intentions and not get distracted by bullshit. I wouldn't be afraid to be vulnerable and talk about how I had to mess everything up in order to find my way.

I applied immediately and danced with excitement when I was called in for the interview. I would have multiple interviews in one day and I would have to prepare for a public presentation open to everyone on campus.

Madison became my audience and helped me tweak my job talk. I had to convince them I was only side-tracked for the past four years. I had no business being the assistant to the numero uno vice-president. It was not my passion. However, I had worked well with college students in the past. I knew that was something I could do with joy and energy.

Surprisingly, I was not devastated when I was not offered the position. I was told it was a difficult decision between me and another candidate. The candidate who did not spend the last four years of her life staggering through the wilderness was offered the job. I accepted their decision. It made sense. As a result of going through those steps and reflecting on my deepest passions, I regained my sense of purpose. Madison was absolutely correct—I had to finish my book and I had to find new way to make a living while making a life.

I talked to a career professional at the university where I was still employed. I shared with her my interest in moving into the field and asked what would she recommend I do. She suggested I start by enrolling in the career development class offered at our university. I did just that. Learning about the need for fulfilling work only solidified my own plans.

In the meantime, I kept the writing goal alive by applying for writing fellowships in town. I was accepted into two of them. It all kept me extremely busy, taking the class, participating in intense writing programs, while still working at the university for the head VP.

Madison, friends, babysitters, and my brother Kyle would all spend time with kids while I engaged in the process of changing my existence. Months after I had been brought back to life and began moving toward my plans, I received a call from the hiring manager for the position I was not offered. The position was vacant once again, and he wondered if I might still be interested. By that time, I wasn't sure if it was the right step, but I stepped into the role anyway.

At the same time, I stayed committed to writing. I was awarded two writing grants. I wrote multiple drafts of the same story, trying to make sense of it. The day we met for lunch eight years ago, Madison stood at the bottom of the landing with her shoulder propped up against the antique-white cinderblock. Her posture was relaxed, but her face told another story. Did she wonder if my purpose for lunch concurred with her purpose? Did she oscillate between her logical left and emotional right?

Loving me was against her logical left. Luckily, she did posses an emotional right. Eight years later, I am grateful that Madison did not give into my demands. I was left with no choice but to do the hardest thing I had ever done on my own—raise JB and Jodi—all the while not letting go of my personal desires to create a life I am proud to live and finishing my book. Done. Done, done, done.

Sherrie Fernandez-Williams is the author of *Soft*. She holds an MFA in Writing from Hamline University in Saint Paul, Minnesota, and is the recipient of an Artist Initiative Award through the Minnesota State Arts Board as well as a SASE/Jerome Grant through Intermedia Arts of Minneapolis. She was a Loft Mentor Series winner for Creative Nonfiction, selected for a Givens Black Writers Collaborative Retreat, and received a Jones Commission Award for new playwrights through the Playwrights' Center of Minneapolis. Excerpts of her memoir have been published in several literary journals and anthologies. Fernandez-Williams discovered her need for words in Brooklyn, New York, where she was born and raised, but she "grew up" as a writer in Twin Cities. She resides and teaches in Saint Paul, Minnesota.

Author photo courtesy of M.K. Smith.